Digitalization of Financial Services in the Age of Cloud

Considerations for Your Organization's Cloud Strategy

Jamil Mina, Armin Warda, Rafael Marins, and Russ Miles

Beijing · Boston · Farnham · Sebastopol · Tokyo

Contents

Preface

Don't believe the (cloud) hype. Even when we limit the scope to financial services when it comes to strategy, there is no "one way." We know that now, and we've known it for several hundred years.

Why We Wrote This Book

In the late Renaissance, a shift in thinking occurred. Magic and mysticism shuffled into the background, and the scientific perspective and method took hold. Hopes and prayers took a step back, and careful, and sometimes not-so-careful, experimental progress took its moment in the limelight.

In this book, we aim to achieve the same thing on a more modest scale. Countering the myths created by victims of hindsight bias or, worse, vendor-induced overpromises, we wrote this book as a navigational aid to help you avoid the Bermuda Triangle of naive change and instead plot a scientific course to the much-desired return on investment (ROI) of digitalization in the age of the cloud.

We don't pretend there is one journey to rule them all. Digitalization, as you'll learn from the get-go, is a complex, sociotechnical evolution that will disrupt your systems and processes. Your journey will be unique, and in this book, we show you how to construct and, iteratively and incrementally, execute a roadmap toward the ROI you seek. It's your company's money and your decisions to make; we help you build a strategy and roadmap based on scientific experimentation to give you the best chance of reaching your destination.

Your journey to digitalization ROI is made up of careful experimental steps, and our goal is for this to be the book that helps you construct the map you need.

How to Use (or Navigate) This Book

We've split this book into three parts. The first part deals squarely with what digitalization is, how and what a strategy is, and how everything ties back to the ROI signals you are seeking.

Part II leaps from theoretical foundations into the financial services context. Several of the key forces in the sector are explored as important context to your strategic deliberations. Now you are ready for Part III, where you get to pick, choose, and generally jump among different categories of change to decide on the experimental templates you might incorporate into your roadmap to gain your own digitalization ROI in the cloud.

Supplemental Material

Supplemental material (experiment templates, etc.) is available for download at *https:// oreil.ly/dfsac_experiments*.

If you have a question, please send email to *support@oreilly.com*.

We appreciate, but generally do not require, attribution. An attribution usually includes the title, author, publisher, and ISBN. For example: *"Digitalization of Financial Services in the Age of Cloud* by Jamil Mina, Armin Warda, Rafael Marins, and Russ Miles (O'Reilly). Copyright O'Reilly Media Inc., 978-1-098-13627-7."

If you feel your use of code examples falls outside fair use or the permission given above, feel free to contact us at *permissions@oreilly.com*.

O'Reilly Online Learning

 For more than 40 years, *O'Reilly Media* has provided technology and business training, knowledge, and insight to help companies succeed.

Our unique network of experts and innovators share their knowledge and expertise through books, articles, and our online learning platform. O'Reilly's online learning platform gives you on-demand access to live training courses, in-depth learning paths, interactive coding environments, and a vast collection of text and video from O'Reilly and 200+ other publishers. For more information, visit *https://oreilly.com*.

How to Contact Us

Please address comments and questions concerning this book to the publisher:

O'Reilly Media, Inc.

1005 Gravenstein Highway North

Sebastopol, CA 95472

800-889-8969 (in the United States or Canada)

707-829-7019 (international or local)

707-829-0104 (fax)

support@oreilly.com

https://www.oreilly.com/about/contact.html

We have a web page for this book, where we list errata, examples, and any additional information. You can access this page at *https://oreil.ly/DFS_cloud*.

For news and information about our books and courses, visit *https://oreilly.com*.

Find us on LinkedIn: *https://linkedin.com/company/oreilly-media.*
Follow us on Twitter: *https://twitter.com/oreillymedia.*
Watch us on YouTube: *https://www.youtube.com/oreillymedia.*

Acknowledgments

The authors would like to express sincere gratitude to the many individuals who contributed to this book. The technical reviewers and editorial team provided invaluable insights, working tirelessly to ensure our work was accurate, accessible, and engaging to readers. We could not have done this without your dedication and hard work.

A special thanks to Fiona McNeill, whose participation was instrumental in making this work possible. Just as the passage of a comet can bring together spectators and expectations (of a lifetime), Fiona's vision and foresight were key to transforming scattered experiences and expertise into a cohesive and meaningful result. She generously donated her time and expertise to sort out the details and inspire us to do hard work with passion. We are grateful for her dedication and generosity and feel fortunate to have had her guidance and support throughout this journey.

JAMIL MINA

The first thing that comes to my mind as I write this acknowledgment is that Fiona McNeill is very passionate about the people who work with her and about building a community of like-minded individuals. She brought us together as a team from across the globe to collaborate on a topic that we are all passionate about. We want to give special recognition of her foresight, leadership, and steady hand in management. As she heads into retirement, she will always be remembered as a friend.

ARMIN WARDA

I'd like to thank all my coworkers at Red Hat for creating such an inspiring, open, inclusive working environment. Discussions with customers have been very valuable in understanding the needs and priorities of financial services companies in their cloud journey. Our global system integration partners have contributed a lot of business knowledge to these discussions.

My special thanks go to my wife and family for their love and care, for supporting my flexible working style, and for enduring my comments on events reported in the mainstream media with respect to financial services, digitalization, data privacy, digital sovereignty, and artificial intelligence. I also want to thank my cycling buddies for supporting me in our shared hobby that helps me to keep my mental balance.

RAFAEL MARINS

Life is full of surprises and offers us incredible opportunities to explore paths we never imagined. I am immensely grateful to everyone who has joined me on my journey. Special recognition goes to my dedicated teammates Eric Marts, Fiona McNeill, and Jeff Picozzi. This book reflects our countless conversations and diligent efforts in addressing customer needs.

As it couldn't be any different, I would like to express my profound gratitude to my parents, Valmir and Célia, for shaping me into a whole and fulfilled individual. Your guidance and teachings have instilled in me the courage to ask questions, pursue knowledge, and maintain an open mind to life's possibilities.

To my wife, Daniele, your generosity and unwavering support have brought us this far and will continue to strengthen our bond. To my children—Thalia, Davi, and Anna Sophie—you are life's most precious gifts. It is an honor to watch you grow and flourish and to see love and wisdom enrich our lives with grace. Thank you all for your patience, support, and for being an integral part of me and my journey.

RUSS MILES

Writing acknowledgments is enormous fun and fraught with peril. Never in the field of writing do you get such a chance to endear yourselves to so few and upset so many. Well unless you write for a British tabloid. To those I've remembered, thank you. To those I've forgotten, I'm sorry, and I'm sure you'll remind me of it for the rest of my life. Love to you all.

Firstly, always, I'd like to acknowledge my family: Mali; Sophie; Mum and Dad; Bobs, Ad, Isla, Amber, and Lucky; Rich, Jo, Teddy, Luke, and Leia. You all know you're fabulous and that I owe a massive debt for your sufferance of me.

Thanks especially also to people who have been more than friends to me: Monica, Emma, and Andy; Jo and Monty; Nicky and Graham; and Chris and Nadia. Thanks to Olga, Adrian, and my family at Amazon and AWS. You've all been there when life was at its toughest, and I look forward to so many more moments in better times ahead!

Thanks to my incredible team at Crown Agents Bank. You've been such an inspiration and honor to work alongside, and your support in those dark days in the middle of the writing process will never, ever be forgotten.

Next, my O'Reilly family. You are all the best of the best, and it's always a privilege to work with you. Especially to Melissa and Gary—there were times when I wasn't even sure if I was going to live long enough to complete this book, but you both believed in me. Gary, you are an incredible editor, and your belief in my writing style has taught me again the joy of writing. I'll miss laughing with you on a weekly basis as I excitedly present a new, harebrained way to explain a complex concept with a broken metaphor. Here's to many more opportunities to work together!

A huge thanks also to the wonderful team at Red Hat, whose patience with how the book evolved and emerged was and is hugely appreciated!

Finally, I want to thank all the staff at the Sussex Cancer Centre, and especially my awesome Macmillan[1] nurse, Hannah Friend. I started this book in the middle of radiotherapy and chemotherapy treatments, and now I finish it gratefully cancer-free. You are all absolute angels-sans-wings, and I will always be grateful for the service you provided to me. It meant, and continues to mean, the world.

---

1 Macmillan Cancer Support (*https://www.macmillan.org.uk*)

PART I

Digitalization and Cloud Strategy

Strategy and Digitalization

"Strategy is the art of manipulating an environment to gain a desirable outcome."

—*Simon Wardley, researcher and creator of Wardley Mapping*

This book helps you build a successful technology strategy for digitalization in a financial services organization. When I (Russ) hear the word *strategy*, I tend to think of a blurrily defined set of ideas, often captured on PowerPoint slides that simultaneously manage to have too much and too little information on them. Strategies of this sort are usually combined with a power lunch, handwaving and applause, and lots of nodding followed by a concerted effort to ignore those slides for another year of manic work activity. I used to think strategy was where bad ideas go to die.

Not anymore. Strategy *can* be the difference between an organization's life and (slow) death. For organizations that have almost entirely nailed their colors to technology, such as financial services, a technology strategy becomes not where good ideas go to die but where crucial discussions and actions go to live.

What Is Strategy?

At the risk of explaining one hard-to-pin-down term with a set of others, *strategy* is *situational awareness* and *anticipation* of the future, combined with *decision making*, packaged up in a healthy loop of *learning*. Strategy is what you use to decide how to play a game, in our case the game of investment in technology. Your technology strategy captures your complex *environment* from a technology perspective and then your *decisions* about how you want to use it and what moves you want to make, smartly spending your precious resources.

To build your strategy, you need to ask:

What's the purpose of the game?
> What does winning look like? Who are you trying to satisfy? Usually this is some sort of important stakeholder, like your customer.

What does the situation look like?

What is the context-specific environment? What is the value stream, or compo nents, that satisfies the needs of the stakeholders? What are the different stages o evolution for each component (genesis, custom build, product, commodity)? Wha forces of nature or economic drivers, sometimes called climatic patterns, influenc the situation?

What can be expected from the future?

Are there any technology trends, new requirements, or changing customer expect ations in play? Will the business, the organization, or the technology budget grov or shrink? Are we confronted with new regulations? Do we see new competition New partners?

Where should you direct yourself?

Are there any general rules or guidance that help you play the game smarter? Ar there any general principles you can follow to point yourself in the right direction setting the frame for what questions need to be answered?

What do you need to decide?

What are the key decisions you need to make to get things moving? How will you define the priorities? What do you need to decide in order to...

Act!

In addition to capturing the situation, getting pointed in the right direction, and deciding to act, it's important to use your work on strategy to *learn and adapt*. A strategy shouldn't be a once-a-year document to be prettied up in PowerPoint and used at annua meetings; although it can be used for those purposes, it is a living document, a continua draft. It is a capture of the game and the decisions you make at a point in time that you continually revisit as the game progresses, refining and learning from so that you can become a better player and give yourself the best chance of winning.

The Purpose of Digitalization

If strategy is how you explore the game space and plan to play, all questions start with "How do we win?" What would success look like? What's the purpose of digitalization. What's the goal of the game?

In financial services, as in many sectors, the purpose is to satisfy your customer's *needs*. By looking carefully at what a customer needs, you can begin to explore the resources, activities, and components (see Part II) that will come into play to meet those needs. You can construct value streams that meet those needs, mapping out the compo nents that make it all possible. This may sound simple. However, it rarely is because the list of stakeholders in financial services, particularly for regulated institutions, is quite complicated—made up of the shareholders, customers and, of course, regulators.

The difficulty is that these stakeholders, and their needs, are constantly jostling for a place at the top of the priority list. Frequently, customer needs are displaced by other goals, such as operational efficiency, the promise of cost savings, etc. Cloud vendors understand this jostling for position in your priorities, which has led to wild promises of easy deliverables of all of the above and more. Hype has led to overpromising and underdelivering and to widespread disillusionment with cloud adoption.

Cloud Adoption Disillusionment

It was somewhat inevitable that we'd become disillusioned with cloud adoption when the expectations, and the promises, were so high. It's complex and therefore difficult to sell a new approach to technology on the basis of being able to meet customer needs more effectively. Much easier is to explain how you will generate massive cost savings by moving away from incumbent data centers. "Shift everything from CapEx to OpEx and save a fortune" was the rallying cry, until it became a whimper.

Another frequent misconception is that applications automagically become modern, cloud-native apps when they are moved to the cloud. But if you move technical debt to the cloud, you will have technical debt in the cloud. That's why most successful cloud adopters accompany their cloud strategy with an app modernization strategy.

Like many overly simplistic strategies, the wholescale movement (and often accompanying redefinition) of existing systems to the cloud has been extremely painful and often yielded little real return on investment—at least within the expected ROI timelines. So much so that whole new terms have been invented, such as "hybrid cloud," to convey that you are doing "cloud," even if you still have some parts of your system residing happily in your own CapEx data centers.

Could this disillusionment have been avoided? Probably, yes. Cloud, like any other technology, comes with advantages and disadvantages. One-size-fits-all works only on PowerPoint slides.

Ill-defined "strategies" such as "digitization" and "cloudification" are of this one-size-fits-all ilk. *Digitization* is the digital conversion of existing processes and artifacts; cloudification is similar in that it is the conversion of existing resources to execute and be stored on the cloud. Digitization's blind transference of existing processes and data into computers, and cloudification's similar approach, just with the destination being other people's computers, has made it hard not to become cynical about the whole sorry mess.

The answer is not to forget who should be at the top of your list of priorities: your customer. The needs of your existing customers, and the future needs of your future customers, are *the* anchor at the heart of your technology strategy. How to evolve your systems to better meet those needs is the first question you need to ask. That's not to say the other priorities, such as cost savings, are not important; they are firmly on the list, and you will see how to factor them into your strategy and roadmaps in the coming chapters. But if we displace the customer as the anchor of our strategies, we run the risk of ending up again with a highly polished system but no real net gain. We end up with disillusionment, again.

Digitalization Versus Digitization (and Cloudification)

If digitization is the digital conversion of existing processes and data, *digitalization* is the digital *transformation* of your processes and data to make them more effective. Digitization and cloudification may have contributed to disillusionment and disappointment, digitalization *should* not.

Note

Don't you have to digitize in order to digitalize?

While digitalization completely relies on digitization, and often cloudification, to conduct the target transformations, the focus is not on simply whether a set of activities, or jobs, can be digitized. Instead digitalization focuses on what a more effective set of processes might be when a stakeholder's need can be met using digital technologies.

Digitalization encourages us to create a strategy and resulting roadmaps that transform our existing investment in technology rather than merely mimic what happened before. By asking what is important to better serve your *digitalization strategy anchor points*, you can transform your existing systems toward better serving those anchor points.

Digitalization, Strategy, and Cloud

Digitalization is transformation, but transformation into *what*? The "cloud, of course" answer has been shown to lead to disillusionment through blind cloudification. Cloud gives us meaningful advantages in the right *contexts*, and for specific *reasons*, and strategy is the tool that helps us explore those reasons and contexts.

Asking hard questions, exploring complex options, and understanding what this all could mean in your unique context, all while looking through the lens of what matters to you and your organization, are the components of a great digitalization strategy. Doing this hard thinking is the difference between real value and sunk cost, and this is the hard work that this book is going to help you do.

Getting Started: Parts of a Digitalization Strategy

Earlier we mentioned that a strategy is developed by exploring several questions:

- What's the *purpose* of the game?
- What does the situation look like?
- What's ahead?
- Where could you direct yourself?
- What do you need to decide?
- Act!

Let's now make that more digitalization-centric:

- What's the *purpose* of your digitalization?
- What does the situation currently look like?
- Where could you direct your resources?
- What do you need to decide, and when?
- Go do it, and gather feedback regularly so you can learn, improve, and refine every facet of your strategy, including your purpose.

Savvy strategists may have noticed that these questions are a rephrasing of John R. Boyd's OODA loop, as shown in Figure 1-1.

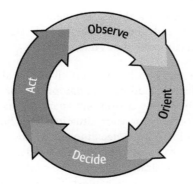

Figure 1-1. A simplified view of John Boyd's OODA loop

Observe
> Observe the game you are building a strategy for. Gather as much knowledge from as many parties as possible to help quickly describe the current situation. What does the landscape look like, and what forces out of your control are acting on that landscape?

Orient
> What plays in the playbook could you apply to the situation? Are there any quick wins, now that you have a grip on the game board you're playing on?

Decide
> It's time to get specific and decide what actions you are going to take, factoring in the appropriate plays you recognize you could make along with the situation you've surfaced.

Act
> Go do it! And, just as importantly, learn from what happens and build your knowledge of the situation so you can go around the loop again.

Starting from your purpose (i.e., what success looks like for your digitalization transformation), each of these phases of your strategy cycle has a focus:

Observe → **Landscape and climate**

What is the current state of your systems? Who matters most—who are you trying to serve according to the purpose of your digitalization? How do the systems currently collaborate and depend on one another to provide those services and meet those needs?

Orient → **Doctrine**

Are you focusing on real users, stakeholders, and needs? Is cost the primary priority? What is your approach to quality? How should you balance your risks?

Decide & Act → **Leadership**

Could shifting a system to a third party deliver real benefits? How fast does a system need to adapt, and under whose control? Do the benefits of cloud really matter to this system component or value stream?

In this book, you are going to learn to do all of the above to create a successful digitalization strategy, utilizing cloud where appropriate, for your system and business. You'll explore how to capture your current situation, the hard-earned lessons that you can consider applicable doctrine for your situation, and how to navigate the various important questions you will face when deciding exactly how to transform your situation.

In the coming chapters, we'll look to eliminate the danger of cloud disillusionment, instead building a digitalization strategy that you are confident will deliver the benefits of cloud, where appropriate, to your unique context. The first step is to capture your current situation: your market landscape and your business climate.

Starting with the End in Mind

Naive digitization was so frequently a bad return on investment precisely because it didn't focus on transforming the business processes. This is where digitalization's opportunity arises—imagining how your chains of value can leverage the promise of technology, in particular cloud technologies, creating an opportunity for real, tangible returns on investment.

The opportunity, of course, needs to be balanced with greater risk. Every aspect of your strategy will be a trade-off between various returns on investment. The potential for higher returns in digitalization comes with a greater risk of missing the mark. In this chapter, you will explore how to start with the goal in mind, what your digitalization strategy will deliver, and how you will then be able to rapidly iterate across your value chains as you look to manifest that value.

Show Me the Return on Investment (ROI)!

Digitalization starts with a different question than digitization:

> While digitization *refers to the act of making analog information digital,* digitalization *is all about moving existing processes into digital technologies. In other words,* digitization *is for information, whereas* digitalization *is for processes.*
>
> —Kihara Kimachia, "What Is Digitization vs. Digitalization vs. Digital Transformation?" (https://oreil.ly/ll81u)

Digitization began with "How can we leverage technology to digitize our existing business documents and automate their processing?" Digitalization is founded on the question "How can our business processes and value chains themselves evolve to make the most of technology?"

One starting point is to ask how your systems should be better after your digitalization investment. What will your business be capable of that it couldn't do before, or couldn't do *easily* before, and why is that important to your chances of success as a financial services business? How can you evolve your business value chains so they are successful *because of* enabling technology rather than *in spite of* technology?

Digitalization's return on investment begins most powerfully with that last question. What changes can you make that will help your business turn technology from a source of inertia into one of momentum?

We can't answer all those questions for your unique context in this book, but we can help you understand the factors to consider. We can lay out which technology levers may become available to you and how to explore what you have and what you could achieve. This all begins with considering your business's value chains.

Value Chains and Business Perspectives

A value chain is a set of components, often systems in themselves, connected across your business that depend on one another to meet a specific business need from a specific business perspective.

Note

Value chains should not be confused with value streams. A *value chain* is the set of components that collectively support the provision of some value, whereas a *value stream* is the processes that take place, in a particular order, when delivering that value.

The perspectives that you consider in your value chain could be those of anyone in your organization, but typically you will take on the perspectives of your end users, customers, or other important business stakeholders. An example might be a value chain that supports the customer's ability to view an account balance, as shown in Figure 2-. The figure is based on an example from our recent experience; your value chains may look quite different!

In Figure 2-1, the value chain is designed to meet the customer's need to view account balances. The chain is composed of interdependent components including the account ledger, which manages the golden copy of account statuses; the Identity system, which manages and validates the user identity; their joint dependence on being hosted in a data center, and the dependency of the data center on the local power grid.

In this way, you can begin to use value chains to surface, share awareness of, and discuss the dependencies necessary to support important business processes and different perspectives on the needs of those processes. Each value chain can be examined to decide what capabilities it needs to provide and, perhaps more importantly, how they could be redesigned to improve efficiency and effectiveness—perhaps even to unlock new value chains altogether.

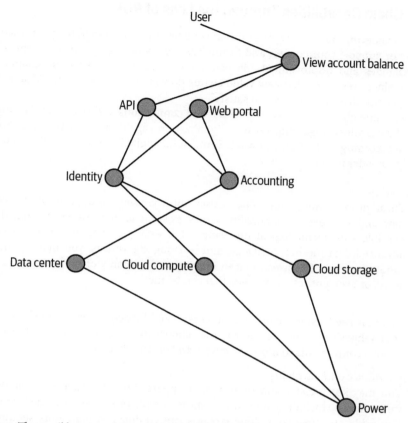

Figure 2-1. The possible components and their dependencies in a value chain designed to show customers their account balances

Note

Your customers' perspectives are not the only ones served by your value chains. As you begin to map out your value chains (discussed in Chapter 3, "Mapping the Landscape"), you will surface, dream up, and improve many different value chains across your business as you explore what you'd change as part of your digitalization strategy. Typical examples of teams that can benefit from modifying value chains might include shareholders, regulatory organizations, risk officers, and even engineering and operations teams.

Value Chain Capabilities Through the Lens of ROI

When considering how you want to invest your resources to transform your systems so they better support your current and future business, you begin with your value chains. What changes and improvements do you want to make to those value chains to get better business results? What new value chains do you want to establish? What new and existing perspectives do you need to satisfy?

Each value chain, and the components and connections and systems it is composed of, can be examined regarding various digitalization capabilities that you can choose to invest in according to the ROI you want. Some of the digitalization capabilities you would typically consider include:

Functionality
> Through examining your value chains, you may see the opportunity to invest in new and improved functionality across existing or new value streams that are possible with technological innovation. For example, with technologies such as advanced data meshes, analytics, and learning algorithms, you may see new and innovative cases for investment in improving the quality of the current needs you serve, or even entirely new needs that can be met.

Agility
> You may see friction, redundant processes, and inadequate speed of change across your value chains. As a result, you may choose to invest in improving the agility of various components to more effectively and efficiently meet changing needs.

Data governance and durability
> You may see broader and more potent opportunities for data usage across your value chains, including how your data is stored, protected, governed, and made accessible and how your value streams can conform to regulatory requirements without sacrificing capabilities such as agility and scalability.

Operability
> You may see opportunities to improve operational efficiency and resiliency across your value chains.

Scalability
> You may see the need to rethink the components of your value chains to enhance speed to market by making components reusable or by supporting larger workforces to contribute to them. You may also see ways that a value chain can satisfy new and larger volumes of demand.

Security
> You may see opportunities to invest in new security approaches across existing and new value chains to gain from economies of scale, commoditization, and speed of change without sacrificing security.

Availability
> Your value chains must be ready on request when the user expects or needs them to be. If those expectations and needs are not met, or if they could be relaxed, then this is an area to consider for investment.

Reliability
> Through examining and discussing the needs of your value chains, you may discover opportunities to improve their reliability, availability, and even resilience in the face of changing, turbulent conditions, thereby mitigating risk.

Learnability
> The ability to change direction with agility and scale when needed is most valuable when paired with learning which value chains are proving successful and which need attention or, perhaps, retirement. To make better business decisions, you might choose to invest in strong feedback and learning loops in your organization.

Financial services value chains come with some additional investment priorities:

Regulatory environment and compliance
> As you establish and evolve your value chains, you will naturally need to consider and comply with the ever-evolving regulations and laws that your organization needs to adhere to. Key examples include traceability, auditability, and explainability of the behavior throughout your value chains.

In addition to these capabilities, you may be able to capture and describe others that you will choose to invest in as part of your digitalization initiative. The key goal is to leverage and *evolve* your value chains to get real, ideally measurable, ROI from the capabilities you carefully choose to focus on. These will then filter the possibilities you choose to incorporate into your digitalization.

Gathering the Right Perspectives

Several perspectives are needed to help you decide what mix of capabilities, applied to which components of your existing and planned value streams, represent a good ROI for your digitalization journey. You will likely consult with the following:

Technology community
> By including the actual developers, testers, and architects in the early stages of planning for your digitalization, you will be able to listen to and incorporate the real concerns of those who are responsible for the technical systems and who will likely most benefit from and leverage the changes that you look to make.

Platform engineering and operations
> Whether it be your engineering teams, as in DevOps, or separate technical and business operations groups, getting perspectives on the operation and engineering of common platforms across value chains is a crucial sanity check on any ideas that might affect your value chains' operational resilience and performance.

Risk, security, and compliance

Risk mitigation is at the heart of how financial services institutions do business. S this perspective needs to be brought in early to ensure discussion of any propose changes through the lens of the various categories of risk.

Human resources and employee enablement

Evolving value chains can result in a profound shift in the people, aptitude skills, and expertise needed to establish and maintain those chains. Everythir from learning, upskilling, and recruitment program strategies to compensatio and budgetary requirements needs to be factored in by collaborating closely wit talent management teams.

"Friends and family"

Subsets of users or customers who are willing to try new applications, functiona ity, and processes can be invaluable sources of feedback. Who can be beta teste or review mock-ups?

Executive sponsors

These leaders support and promote digitalization initiatives within you organization.

By bringing together people across all of the above roles, and possibly others well, you will gather their important perspectives on the ideal mixture of ROI from you digitalization efforts. Not all perspectives will be equal, but they will all be useful. The a of this exercise will be for you to navigate and distill their sensitivities, opinions, gap and challenges to construct a plan to evolve your value chains to yield maximum ROI fo your business.

Establish Your Strategy Quickly, Reevaluate Continuously

Focusing on the impact on your business's value chains at the heart of your digitalizatio strategy is important. You should be able to evaluate your value chains quickly—and, ju as quickly, evolve your evaluating, revisiting your strategy *frequently* (i.e., at least once quarter).

The cadence for revisiting and revising your digitalization strategy is important t your success because of the nature and complexity of the components and systems i your value chains (not to mention rapidly changing market conditions). If those compo nents were purely technical, then they probably wouldn't be as complex but would b merely complicated.[1]

Your business's value chains consist of technology *and* the people, processes, an practices that create and maintain them—your value chains will be *sociotechnical* i nature as they depend on both technology and social systems. In a very few cases, yo may be able to work with a value chain with clear, well-understood, and fixed constraint

---

1 How you make sense of, and work with, a given context is very different if it is clear, complicated, complex, or chaotic. See the Cynefin framework (*https://oreil.ly/zS1J8*).

In those circumstances, best practices may be evident and can even be lifted and shifted with some confidence from other value chains and systems.

More often, though, the value chains you are looking to establish and evolve as part of your digitalization will be sufficiently complicated and complex that you will not be able to make decisions about them in such a straightforward manner. For the majority of sociotechnical value chains, you will find benefit in an iterative approach of probing, sensing, and responding as you continually reevaluate your strategy and its priority trade-offs, removing blockers along the way. This approach echoes that of Agile methods.

Note

Socio-what?

The term *sociotechnical* is used to describe any system that is composed of technology and people. It encompasses all of the technical facets of a system, from infrastructure through platforms to custom software services, and all of the social facets, including people, politics, routines, practices, and processes.

Combining the mutually collaborative elements of the social systems with the technical systems lets you get a truer picture of how a system operates than if you looked at a system through the two lenses of technology or social aspects in isolation.

Collecting the Parts of Your Digitalization Strategy

While the details of your own strategy are likely to be extremely context specific, in this chapter you've seen how an iterative, experimental, strategic approach will enable you to explore the ROI you are looking for and how your value chains might be created or evolved to better serve your business through technology. You've also seen that, thanks to the complexity likely present in your value chains, any step you take should be evaluated continually against the ROI you are looking to achieve.

This is a good start, but how do you go about building a cloud strategy? What do you need to consider before you can begin carefully exploring and experimenting toward your ROI goals? In Parts II and III of this book, you'll explore the tools you'll need to begin building your cloud strategy based on your own experiments and target returns on investment.

In Part II, "Financial Services Digitalization in Context: Landscape and Climate", you'll start building your strategy by capturing what is currently in place and the forces outside your control that act upon it. You'll learn how to build awareness of the context that your value chains inhabit and, over time, adjust this context as it evolves and you reevaluate your strategy.

Then in Part III, you'll learn that *doctrine* is a collection of common experimental "moves" for you to consider for your digitalization strategy. Some recommendations are small and so come with small risk and rapid feedback. Others may be radical departures from the state of your current systems. This means you'll get slower feedback and thus incur a higher risk of investing, without being able to measure movement toward your target ROI.

The collection of doctrines presented here is a starting point for you to consider for your digitalization strategy. While no doctrine can claim to be exhaustive, the options in these pages represent some of the most typical choices you could make as you feel your way toward your ROI trade-offs.

PART II

Financial Services Digitalization in Context: Landscape and Climate

Mapping the Landscape

"The time you want the map...is before you enter the woods."

—Brendon Burchard, motivation and performance expert

f you were visiting an unfamiliar city, the first thing you'd likely do is check out recommendations online and review some maps of the area. You might check out a street map to get an idea of some distances between your potential accommodation options and the sights you want to see. You might then grab a totally different map to see what transport options are available. And now you glumly conclude that your hotel is miles from anything remotely interesting.

You wouldn't start by jumping on a plane and then just winging it on arrival. You also probably wouldn't just take a stranger's recommendation on faith.

Instead, you'd come up with a high-level idea of what activities and sites are important to you, make sure to prioritize them, and then explore how you could make those things happen. You'd gather intelligence on the location to feel some level of confidence you're going to have a great time when you get there.

"Gathering intelligence" might sound a bit military, but that's actually on purpose. You're doing very much the same thing as a military commander using recon to figure out a strategy. You gather information and develop your skills, awareness, and familiarity with the territory to make the most of your vacation.

Whether you're planning a special forces op, a short city break, or an organizational transformation to meet a current or new customer need, the same steps work. If strategy is the science of exploring what steps to take for the long term, with a vision of what final success would look like, then the first step is to understand what is right there at our feet.

Digitalization is a journey, and every journey should begin with making a map. Before you can start exploring how you want to evolve your systems to take advantage of digitalization, you need to develop a useful picture of the sociotechnical systems you currently have. That might sound straightforward, even obvious, but the trick is not only to understand what you have but also to capture the right intelligence on the context in which it sits and what use it serves. Then you validate its use for the long-term journey. It's time to start building your maps.

Mapping the Situation

As you learned in Chapter 1, the first step toward building your digitalization stra
is to *observe* what you currently have, and it's important to do that in relation to
individual system's context—context such as where the system sits in relation to
other systems it works with and how its place relates to delivering value to the u
the customer, and the organization. Ignoring the complexities of the environmen
which one aspect of your technology investment operates is a shortcut to the woe
digitization and cloudification. To help you make the best strategic decisions, *contex*
king.

Your progress from observation to orientation requires an understanding of
terrain and how your systems relate to it. You need a picture of the current situation,
where you want to go, to know what direction to head in and what changes to conside
part of your digitalization. An abstraction can help you make good decisions in cont
One popular option is a *Wardley Map*.

What Is a Wardley Map?

Simon Wardley originally created Wardley Mapping (*https://learnwardleymapping.co*
simply referred to as *mapping* going forward, as a way to help build strategies that v
not just blind copies of what others were doing. Treating strategy as a game, mapp
gives you a way to capture your specific board and plan your next moves.

At its simplest, a Wardley map surfaces:

An anchor
> The purpose of your digitalization transformation. Most often this involves m
> ing current and new users' current and new needs.

Value chains
> Your system components that interact to meet the user's needs.

Evolution
> The state of evolution of each system component on the map.

Figure 3-1 shows the layout of these concepts on an abstract Wardley Map.

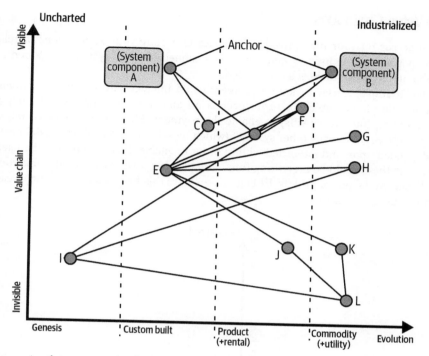

Figure 3-1. An abstract example of a Wardley Map to demonstrate the key concepts involved

Your Anchor and Your System Components

Everything on a map is placed in relation to the *anchor*. Think of the anchor as being the ultimate benefactor of the value that the chain delivers. Space matters on a map, and a system component's position relative to the anchor and the two axes of the map are meaningful too.

In Figure 3-1's abstract example, the anchor is shown to be a user who has needs that are satisfied by certain capabilities. If they had the capabilities (the product, the documentation, the skills, processes, and so on), labeled A through L, then the needs of the user would be met. As the relationships between capabilities and components are defined, the value chain becomes an interconnected system. The anchor is typically placed at the top of the map.

Components A and B are connected too, and to satisfy the needs of the user/anchor, these components depend upon various layers of connected capabilities.

The Value Chain Axis

The first axis on your map provides the space to explore your value chains in relation to the position of the user. A value chain is a connected set of system components that collaborate, typically, to meet a user's needs.

For example, a user making a payment could interact with an app component on their mobile phone, which in turn depends on and interacts with several application programming interfaces (APIs) to enable the payment. Moving farther down the value chain, there may be many other systems (which have their own distinct capabilities) that are depended upon and interacted with in order to enable the payment that the user has instigated; these could be everything from core banking systems, to cloud infrastructure, to reliance on the power grid itself! Figure 3-2 shows this first axis on your map, ready to lay out your value streams.

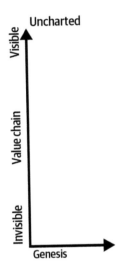

Figure 3-2. The value chain y-axis on your map provides space to lay out the webs of connected systems that collaborate and communicate to meet a user's needs.

The value chain y-axis plots the *visibility* of a component in relation to the user. one end of the value chain axis are the systems (or applications) that the user direct interacts with. These could be user interfaces such as mobile applications and web us interfaces, even APIs. These are system components that are *highly visible* to your use anchor.

Moving further down the axis, you will add capabilities that support the less direc visible components. For example, you may add aspects like internal APIs, third-pa systems, and eventually, as you move down the value chain, low-level infrastructu services and underlying platforms. As you move farther away from the anchor, syste components become less visible to the user.

The value chain axis gives you the space to plot an interdependent web of components and capabilities that spread out from the highly visible components that the user sees and interacts with to the underlying system components that may be entirely invisible to the user, but that are crucial through dependency to meeting their needs.

From Uncharted to Industrialized

While the value chain y-axis gives you the space to plot how your system components collaborate to deliver on a user's need, the horizontal x-axis focuses on how those components themselves *evolve*. As shown in Figure 3-3, this axis typically has four phases that a system component can inhabit: genesis, custom built, product (including rental approaches), and commodity (including utilities).

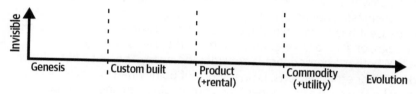

Figure 3-3. Stages of technology evolution are plotted on a map's horizontal axis.

Genesis

Explorative system components found here are unique and high risk because they are rare and unknown. These are the novel capabilities, or they require limited specialist skills to explore and develop, and are constantly changing as they become better understood or more widely adopted.

Custom built

These are still undergoing rapid change, meeting needs in a custom, possibly differentiating, way. There may be one and only one of these types of capabilities in existence. Again, a high degree of specialist skill from developers and maintainers is often needed to maintain and evolve in this phase.

Product (+rental)

Here are the well-defined, understood, more predictable capabilities. These are increasingly stable and can be maintained with slower change. There are alternative options available at this stage of evolution, with the main differentiation being around how well these capabilities do their job.

Commodity (+utility)

These capabilities are standardized, operationally efficient, industrialized, and fit for a specific, well-known purpose; the key differentiators are scale and volume. These are undifferentiated capabilities that don't stand out. They are so prevalent that they become taken for granted.

Across a value chain, components and capabilities on your maps will be at different technological evolution points at a given time. Your strategy will include how you'd like to evolve your components.

Showing a Component Is Legacy?

It can be tempting to think of a component's evolution as progressing naturally through each of the stages across a Wardley Map, and many components, even whole value chains, can follow that trajectory—accidentally or by design. It is natural to then think of all systems evolving this way, and then to consider including further stages in a component's lifecycle such as when the system becomes less fit for the purposes and pressures the business requires of it (i.e., when it is judged as being legacy, perhaps because it has so much technical debt that it cannot be evolved quickly enough, or scaled large enough, to meet the user's needs).

Whether a component is considered "legacy," because of technical debt or for other reasons, is an important point when deciding how to invest and evolve a component, or value chain. Labeling a component "legacy" is an internal colloquial designation, rather than having any relevance to the component's evolutionary stage. A novel and new component can be considered legacy just as easily as a stable, undifferentiating commodity.

Exploring Your Value Chain

The Wardley Map in Figure 3-4, showing a payment and foreign exchange system, is the first of several real-world example maps that we'll refer to throughout the remainder of the book.

In Figure 3-4, the *anchor* is a non-governmental organization (NGO), a category of user that needs to *transfer a payment, perform a foreign exchange trade,* and sometimes do both simultaneously. To enable those components, the system currently has the capabilities affiliated with a web portal, an API, and a foreign exchange system that the user directly interacts with.

Moving away from the user's visibility, other aspects of the system that provide those capabilities come into play. The *foreign exchange (FX)* capability is a self-contained system used by the NGO directly as well as depended on by the payment system. On the x-axis, the FX system depends on a custom data center that, in turn, depends on the power grid at the farthest point on the x-axis. Due to its position on the value chain axis, the power grid capability is the least visible system component to this user.

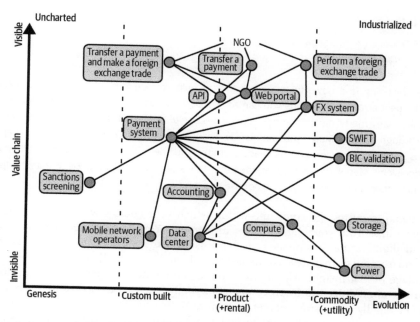

Figure 3-4. An example Wardley Map for a payments and foreign exchange system

On the evolution axis, the map's x-axis, the position of the FX system shows that it is a relatively stable product that is still special to the organization. The data center on the other hand is custom built, and the power grid, as you might expect, is firmly a commodity. Being able to show these different stages of evolution for the various system components becomes crucially important when you are deciding how they might evolve in accordance with your emerging digitalization strategy.

In addition to foreign exchange, a custom-built *payment system* capability provides an *API* and a *web portal*, both placed in the product phase on the evolution x-axis, that the user also interacts with. The payment system then depends on a collection of capabilities to screen, validate, and instruct and settle the payments. Some of those system capabilities are provided "as a service" and are widely available and standardized commodities on the evolution axis, such as integration with the *Society for Worldwide Interbank Financial Telecommunication (SWIFT)* network and *Business Identifier Code (BIC) validation*. Some are products that are not yet standardized, such as *Compute,* and so sit in the product phase on the Evolution axis. Further system capabilities, such as the integration with in-country *mobile network operators* and *sanctions screening*, are highly novel, high risk, and rapidly changing and so are placed in the genesis phase of the evolution axis.

Note

"All models are wrong but some are useful."
　—Simon Wardley

Mapping is a powerful modeling tool to help you explore your context to make the best strategic decisions you can as you digitalize your financial services business. Like many modeling approaches, mapping is *useful* but it does not guarantee success. Through Wardley Maps, you can quickly discuss your own context, fill in as many gaps as you have time for, and be ready to make your decisions—but those are still *your* decisions. Mapping doesn't guarantee that those decisions will be perfect; it just helps make them better than if you did not use mapping.

A map captures the landscape within which your choices will influence the gain you prioritize from your digitalization investment. You could decide that some aspe of your digitalization has opened up the possibility of new and novel users and need and you recognize that new component needs and/or capabilities are needed to tak advantage of that insight. Alternatively, you could identify a capability that is primed become commoditized to improve operational efficiencies, perhaps to be ready to sca to meet rapidly increasing market demands. With your map in hand, you can begi to explore what moves you want to make, influencing your environment to your be advantage.

So far, you've seen the importance of using a map to set out your user's needs, th value chains that meet those needs, and how the constituents of those value chains coul be understood and manipulated to your advantage. Before we dive into the differe moves you could make to adjust your own maps in Part III, it's important to recogniz that *not all moves in the game are being made by you.* There's more to the environmen than just what is under your control. These exogenous forces, called climatic pattern will certainly affect how you decide to shape your value chains.

4

Climatic Patterns in Financial Services

"A change in the weather is sufficient to re-create the world and ourselves."

—Marcel Proust, French novelist

As you explore your value chains, building maps as you go, some factors will come into play that are entirely *out of your control*. Just like the weather, or perhaps more accurately like the climate, these forces and patterns represent additional parameters and constraints that affect how you can evolve and optimize your systems according to the goals of your digitalization strategy. In mapping, these influences on your strategy are called *climatic patterns*.

The Wardley Mapping community is collating an ever-growing catalog of climatic patterns (*https://oreil.ly/6OOtp*) for consideration when building your strategies. Each climatic pattern fits into a defined category. In this chapter, we'll follow the same approach to identify the climatic patterns that are more specific to financial services:

Category	Patterns
Market opportunity	"Financial Services, Everywhere"
Competition	"No Business Is an Island," "Emphasis on Speed, Scale, and Agility"
Components	"Lower Technology Barriers to Entry"
Environmental	"Sustainability Matters"

Climatic Pattern 1: Financial Services, Everywhere

"Financial Services, *Everywhere*" may sound like a cliche, borrowing from slogans fr
the past ("Java Anywhere" anyone?).[1] However, it reflects precisely what financial servi
organizations face today. "Financial Services, Everywhere" is more than catchy mar
ing. It is a fundamental climatic force that is changing in the industry.

The central role of a financial services organization hasn't changed drastically si
people first established financial services products and built their marketplace. On
surface, everything still looks like money. Financial services organizations provide pr
ucts and services that enable money to move, to transform, to grow. But money
just the manifestation, the physical embodiment—in software engineering terms
"concrete API"—of the services provided. Money is the message, but it's not the poin
financial services.

TRUST AND RISK DISTRIBUTION

Every financial services organization deals in something more fundamental than mor
trust and risk distribution. Through reputation, regulation, and daily operation, a fin
cial services organization develops and maintains the trust it needs to provide the ess
tial services individuals and organizations need across the globe.

Services that work within the financial business of that individual or organizat
shoulder the burden of the fundamental risk that the work entails. The global econo
needs to trust financial institutions, and individual people need to trust their finan
institutions. This trust is earned when financial institutions provide the resilience a
risk distribution the economy needs to work at scale and reach, for all parties involved

DIVERSE PRODUCTS, GLOBALLY ACCESSIBLE: EMBEDDED FINANCE

The fundamental remit of financial services has not changed much. But the ways that
job is done, *where* it is done, and how easy and accessible it is have changed beyond
recognition in recent times.

From the very beginning, financial services institutions have taken advantage of 1
technological inventions, innovations, products, and commodity services to bring th
core strengths of trust and risk distribution to their customers. In the early days of
industry, that meant satisfying the needs of the few with capabilities that only a
organizations could provide. Not so anymore.

Nowadays customers expect, and financial services organizations are rushing
supply, financial products and services wherever those customers are—physically
virtually. Platforms are drawing together financial institutions, technology providers, a
distributors of financial products so that those services and products can be *embed
directly into customers' experiences, rather than forcing customers to redirect th
efforts to a financial services institution. More than ever, a customer will choose a s
plier of those products and services from a growing collection of competitors, select

---

1 R. Khare, "W* Effect Considered Harmful [Internet WAP]" (*https://ieeexplore.ieee.org/document/78096.*
IEEE Internet Computing (July–Aug 1999).

one that best meets their needs and can reach them in an increasingly diverse set of physical and virtual, highly convenient locations on demand.

"X, EVERYWHERE" IS A GENERAL CLIMATIC PATTERN

"Financial Services, Everywhere" is not a climatic pattern limited only to financial services. You can see the same market direction in another sector, ecommerce.

Ecommerce is expected to be ubiquitous, and the full spectrum of financial services are being encouraged, even forced, along the same path. This change in customer demand has fueled a rich and evolving ecosystem of digital native FinTechs and other startups that are challenging the hegemony of the traditional financial services organization. In this environment, slow and steady becomes less acceptable when your customers want access to financial services right here, right now, wherever they are and whatever they are doing.

For all these reasons, "Financial Services, Everywhere" has become a crucial market force in the financial services industry. "Financial Services, Everywhere" is our first example of *a climatic pattern* impacting financial services technology strategy, but it is far from being the only one. Next let's leave behind the financial services market and look farther down the value stream at how those "Financial Services, Everywhere" can be supplied.

Climatic Pattern 2: No Business Is an Island

As financial services organizations aim to speedily evolve and supply products and services in more and more diverse locations, the pressure to innovate leads naturally to an "acquire and/or partner" pattern. In an increasingly dynamic environment, incumbent financial institutions become aware of the need to innovate quickly to make the most of existing markets, and reach new ones, while retaining that all-important trusted status.

A fast route to protecting, evolving, and extending your crucial business value chains is either to acquire or insource an existing, complementary technology or partner with a third-party supplier. In financial services, this pattern is most evident in the profusion of financial technology companies that are springing up. Commodity cloud technologies and financial models have successfully lowered the barriers to entry such that a five-person (or fewer!) venture can establish a segment of a financial services value chain valuable enough to augment products by providing their service, entering a formal partnership, or even being acquired.

This pattern is to your advantage if you have prepared an effective digitalization strategy where you know what you have (through your value chain maps), you know what properties you want to achieve and invest in, and you can take advantage of new services/capabilities quickly. Your systems' architecture, and importantly modularity, is the critical factor in making this approach possible. More on this in Chapter 6.

Climatic Pattern 3: Lower Technology Barriers to Entry

It's easy to forget that, in the not-so-distant past, one significant barrier to entry into operating financial services value chains was the investment in technology infrastructure necessary to operate effectively. The computing, networking, and storage capabilities necessary to deliver working, secure, compliant, and reliable capabilities to a segment or complete financial services value chain were expensive enough to represent a significant barrier to entry. A brick-and-mortar presence was crucial to establishing yourself as a financial institution that could be trusted, and indeed interacted with, so the necessary technology tools were available only to the wealthy, established few.

It's true that technical barriers to entry still exist in the form of skills and knowledge. But the walls of technology investment that protected financial institutions from competition in the past have been eroded by the climatic change of large-scale, technology service creation and, in some cases, commoditization. The combination of the largely ubiquitous reach of the internet, universal availability of high-quality, supported, open source–enabling capabilities such as the GNU/Linux operating system, the radial access network for wireless communications, and proliferation of cloud services technology providers means anyone with sufficient, but not necessarily vast, resources can enter the marketplace.

To survive and thrive in the wind of the climatic pattern of commodity cloud computation, you can look in your value chains for opportunities to leverage these economies of scale, rather than banking on resisting them.

Climatic Pattern 4: Emphasis on Speed, Scale, and Agility

Hand in hand with the "Financial Services, Everywhere" pattern goes the need to meet the challenge of increasing competition and innovation in the financial services marketplace. One perspective you can take, and many still do, is to focus on the work necessary to build and maintain your systems, breaking up that work and responsibility into manageable chunks and separating the work, responsibility, and accountability for operating those systems from those responsible for building them.

This approach, sometimes referred to as *siloing*, makes sense when you have well-established, undifferentiated systems that are stable, possibly standardized, and even well-known and replaceable commodities. Slow, steady, long-term iterations of project work may not hinder the evolution of those systems.

For the more specialized, novel, and differentiated systems that form part of your value chains, however, a different approach has emerged as a climatic pattern over the past 20 years. Strengths inherent in the project-focused approach and siloed operations, such as stability and large degrees of change control, have become the very things that make it difficult to react to the changing demands of a market burgeoning with innovative financial services everywhere.

The "Financial Services, Everywhere" pattern means that many system components will be constantly under the relentless pressure to change as they rapidly evolve from early invention and discovery to innovation and, perhaps, stability and commoditization as shown in Figure 4-1.

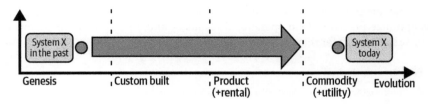

Figure 4-1. A system may begin its life under intense pressure to change in its genesis stage and gradually evolve through being a differentiating product into potentially being a stable utility and commodity in the marketplace.

A different culture and approach are needed for systems earlier in their evolution, and this has manifested as the climatic pattern of "Speed, Scale, and Agility."

As the need for system components and value chains that evolve quickly becomes more apparent, it has been embraced by the teams developing and operating those systems. These teams emphasize the following practices:

Speed
>The capability to deliver change frequently and safely

Agility
>The capability to change direction quickly and easily

Scale
>The capability to be ready to gain economies of scale as the system becomes more stable and well understood by your business and the marketplace

By mapping out your value chains, you can gain insights into where, as part of your digitalization strategy, you will see the need to invest in speed, agility, and scale for particular system components and value chains. These insights will help you organize your people and their responsibilities and accountabilities, along with enabling technologies and practices, optimally to help, not hinder, the unlocking of real value to your business.

Climatic Pattern 5: Sustainability Matters

Given the extreme importance of financial services organizations and the trust placed in them to facilitate so many of the crucial activities of the modern world, it is perhaps unsurprising that the impact of those activities from an environmental standpoint is getting more attention. Ensuring that financial services activities are ecologically sustainable has become a publicly visible priority for ethical and competitive reasons.

As an example of the importance of this climatic pattern, consider how seriously hyperscale cloud service providers, such as Amazon Web Services (AWS), are taking it. AWS launched its "AWS Well-Architected Sustainability Pillar" (*https://oreil.ly/7IISB*) to help teams design and operate value chains while monitoring and optimizing AWS-specific resources and its sustainability metrics (e.g., carbon footprint) to achieve the right sustainable scale and service level to meet users' needs. Other organizations, such as Red Hat, develop a view across multiple hyper-scale cloud resources, helping organizations optimize for cross-cloud operational resiliency and, therefore, optimize for the best mix of sustainability for their value chains.

Note

Beyond sustainability, several other considerations make up what a well-designed and run system and value chain can leverage. You'll explore more of those options, and how to consider them for your own systems and value chains, in Chapters 6 and 8.

Consumers of your services will expect, and demand, that the price of your value chains won't impose an undue environmental cost, so sustainability becomes a consistent challenge to consider as you build your digitalization strategy. Through your strategic choices (see Part III, "Strategic Digitalization Doctrine"), you will balance economic and sustainability factors when selecting the right path for your system components and value streams.

Climatic Patterns Change

As you build your digitalization strategy to get your business's needed ROI, you will keep an eye on the general and specific climatic patterns in play when making choices about how and where you should make investments. You can grow your situational awareness and build your own prioritized catalog of important climatic patterns as you explore your digitalization strategy options.

However, though seemingly part of the firmament, climatic patterns can at times be as changeable as the weather after which they are named.

While sudden changes in the large-scale conditions of your business and marketplace may be rare, they are not without precedent. Therefore, as part of a regular strategic reevaluation, it is a good idea to embrace this potential for change by revisiting your catalog of important climatic patterns to assess whether any have changed in importance or impact or disappeared, or whether entirely new patterns have emerged.

PART III

Strategic Digitalization Doctrine

5

Building Your Digitalization Roadmap

Digitalization is a journey, not a destination, and building your roadmap for that journey, as we mentioned in Chapter 3, is no mean feat. Transforming a complex, sociotechnical domain is not a simple sequence of no-brainer changes. The journey can have twists and turns, as shown on the right in Figure 5-1, and especially given all the power and potential of the cloud, naive changes could easily do more harm than good. There's no digitalization magic wand. Digitalization requires a real roadmap that shows when to evaluate alternative routes, not just a map of a road.

Figure 5-1. What you wish you had to deal with[1] versus what you actually have[2]

Each of your target returns on investment (ROIs) is a property toward which you want to move your value chains and your organization. As shown in Figure 5-2, you know your target ROI, you are aware of the climatic patterns that surround and permeate your systems and the industry, and you know you're dealing with complexity. But how do you know your next step? Where do you start? What do you try first?

---

1 Photo by Diego Jimenez on Unsplash (*https://oreil.ly/WWPwq*).
2 Road in Tibet on the way to Mount Everest Base Camp North. Photo by Russ Miles.

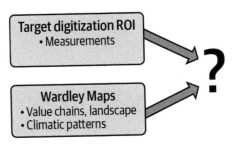

Figure 5-2. You know what you want (target ROI), what you have (landscape of value chains), and what you're dealing with (climatic patterns and your complex sociotechnical system), but what do you do next?

The "Everything, Everywhere, All at Once!" Anti-Pattern

One option is to create a huge initiative involving full-scale transformation; build careful detailed plans for months; and then, when you're ready, and enough stakeholders have signed up in their own arterial blood...go! We call this the "Everything, Everywhere, All at Once!" approach, and it treats digitalization as a discrete project with an all-or-nothing set of goals.

With the right amount of planning, you build confidence that you are going to get the ROI you want. With the right amount of thinking and planning up front, you'll be able to turn that unruly, twisty sociotechnical system into your dream desert highway-straight, clear, and with a good meal at the end of it.

Sadly, this approach just doesn't work for digitalization. You simply can't pick all the winners up front. We all wish it worked this way, but if decades of working with complex system transformation teaches you one thing, it's that everything is a moving target. Everything can and will surprise you, regularly. You may overestimate the capabilities and capacity in your own organization, overreaching and missing the ROI you're looking for. If a cloud agenda is pushed too much, then a rush to the cloud can ensure that also misses important prerequisites to getting the ROI you seek. In a nutshell, the "Everything, Everywhere, All at Once!" approach has failed too many times to be considered seriously.

In the preceding chapters, you've already seen that strategies are best driven in an iterative, incremental way, tightening the OODA loops as much as possible so you can adapt as the system evolves (Figure 5-3). (See "Getting Started: Parts of a Digitalization Strategy" on page 4 for a review of the Observe, Orient, Decide, and Act loops.)

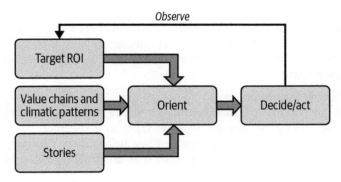

Figure 5-3. Adding OODA to what you want, what you have, and what you're dealing with

Changing everything at once, like a Big Bang, is not going to work—unless the bang you were looking for was unpredictable chaos. Rather than planning a huge program of work, across multiple projects, we've found that it's better to think of your digitalization strategy as a small set of steps that *might*, and only might, move you toward the ROI you're seeking.

Each step, executed in sequence or very carefully in parallel, is a chance to learn more; to see if your target ROI is emerging; and to reflect, refine, and respond differently when you consider your next steps. Each step is a deliverable, and each step is an experiment.

Iterative and Incremental with Experiments

Each step on your digitalization journey is an experiment; each is an attempt to explore whether you are moving toward or away from your target digitalization ROI. Each experiment will describe:

A hypothesis
> This is a statement of the ROI you hope to see signaled when you conduct the experiment. How will you measure signals of ROI, and whose experiences will you gather so you can learn more about the results of the experiment? (See "Learning from Experiments" on page 37.) A seemingly sound hypothesis can be disproved as well as proved, so make sure you incorporate as many opportunities to learn whether ROI is manifesting or not.[3]

---

3 It can be oh-so-tempting to look only for confirmations. *Confirmation bias* is very, very real. While it's not always possible to frame a digitalization experiment as a full, scientific double-blind study, ensuring you engage as much positive and potentially negative feedback as possible is crucial to your digitalization success. That feedback will help you select the best experiments to run next, while undue confirmation will only guide you down the wrong road as you attempt to navigate toward your target ROI.

A method

You need to capture how you are going to conduct the experiment; when you w: know you're done; what signals might indicate that the experiment should er early; and how much the experiment will cost in time, mental bandwidth, and ha cash investment.

An experimental investigation

There's no point doing an experiment if you're not going to learn from it (se "Learning from Experiments" on page 37). Each experiment is not so much success or failure but rather a source of new information. Planning to learn fro the information an experiment presents is as important as planning and runnir the experiment.

Your first step will be to work with your people to build a collection, a *backlog,* *potential* experiments that you believe will help you seek that elusive ROI. Executir digitalization is like a hunt for ROI, and your backlog of experiments is your collection tools that will help you hack through the undergrowth.

Building Your Digitalization Experiment Backlog

Backlogs are not a new concept in Agile software development, where an item in backlog is ideally some iterative deliverable increment of value, which will be a sequence of many, ideally small, experiments in your digitalization backlog. Each experiment a deliverable; each experiment delivers learning as to whether the investment you' making as part of the experiment's method is moving you toward or away from yo target ROI; each experiment is an opportunity to learn, adjust, and adapt the experimen you are planning in the future.

Just like an Agile delivery backlog, your digitalization experiment backlog is a *funne* At the top of the funnel, you will have blurry experiments, perhaps even only vague idea of experiments, and then at the bottom of the funnel, you will have experiments that an ready to be run to unleash the learnings you need (see Figure 5-4).

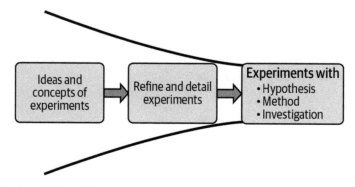

Figure 5-4. The funnel of experiments

You will carefully consider which experiments to refine and detail to the point where they are ready to be run based upon each experiment's hypothetical signals of ROI impact. You will also consider how many, if any, experiments can be executed in tandem and still get valid learnings; it's important to be wary of cross-talk between experiments that gives rise to the "dirty petri dish" problem,[4] where the findings of one experiment could affect the findings from another.

It's worth remembering that an experiment is there to tell you where to double down on your investment if your target ROI is emerging. If you can't tell which experiment led to the signals you're seeing, then you've learned little or nothing.

You'll collate the findings from each experiment in a regular report to stakeholders on the impacts being seen, the evidence of those impacts, and how those learnings will now inform the next set of experiments on your digitalization journey. Those findings, and the decisions they help you make as you evolve your digitalization strategy, are the key to the success of your efforts and the success of your organization's investment.

Learning from Experiments

Experiments are the steps on your digitalization path, each step being an opportunity to reflect, retrospect, learn, and adjust your next steps as you move toward your target ROI. We can now tie the room together by adding your digitalization experiment funnel to your incremental and iterative OODA loop, as shown in Figure 5-5.

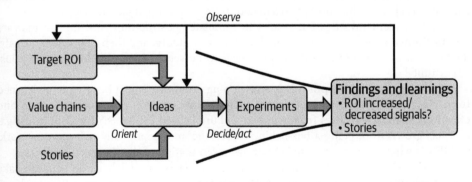

Figure 5-5. Using experiments to observe, learn, and adapt your strategic goals as well as your next experimental steps

---

4 Not everyone is as lucky as Alexander Fleming when working with dirty scientific equipment (*https://oreil.ly/dUDEO*).

THE IMPORTANCE OF STORIES

One element in Figure 5-5 that might surprise you is the "stories."[5] *Stories*, which are one of the key findings you'll use to learn from your experiments, make an appearance as you build your strategy.

Stories capture the impacts of your experiments—they are how we make sense of a complex environment (*https://oreil.ly/_6Utz*). If you focused *only* on the hard data signal of your target ROI, you'd get a fairly impoverished, one-sided, and potentially damaging measurement of how your organization is improving through your digitalization efforts. As an example, the data might be screaming at you that more customers are using a feature you built to meet their need, but when you explore the customers' stories, their perspectives, you find that they are using that feature because the experience of other features is so bad. Stories deliver the richer picture you need, the additional perspective required, to interpret your data with context.

Capturing multiple stakeholders' experiences of your changes by listening to their stories is a crucial part of exploring the real impact of the changes brought about by your experiments. Stories provide the subjective findings that will help you get more ROI from your experiments and then help you make even smarter decisions about future experiments and steps along your path.

LESSONS LEARNED FROM "LEARNING FROM INCIDENTS"

Your experiments are only as valuable as the lessons you can learn from them. This challenge is shared with another area of continuous learning: incident investigations.

Poor incident investigation results in template "postmortem" documents that are rapidly thrown together, quickly signed off for the auditors, and then popped on a dusty digital shelf somewhere in SharePoint, never to be seen again. But this is such a lost opportunity!

Every incident is a surprise! It is a surprising event that is just begging to be learned from. This is why modern methods of incident investigation emphasize creating and effectively sharing learnings from planned and unplanned incidents.[6] Incident investigation has grown from being a box-ticking exercise to an exceptionally rich piece of work, and this is what you can aspire to in your own examination of experimental findings.

Howie (How We got here) (*https://oreil.ly/ApOoL*) is one such guide you can take inspiration from. The Howie guide identifies eight activities to help you gather evidence and stories around: *assign* (the person who is going to lead the investigation), *identify* (the data to be collected), *analyze* (the data iteratively), *interview* (to gather the candid stories), *calibrate* (with everyone involved), *meet* (to discuss and review the findings), and

---

5 Not to be confused with Agile "user stories." Stories here are literally the experiences of other stakeholders with, their perspectives on, the outcomes of experiments. A user story in Agile is typically a concise definition of a feature, but here you are looking for multiple, perhaps verbose, even conflicting perspectives so that those can be factored into your learning from your experiment.

6 Planned incidents include Game Days (*https://oreil.ly/ULGzc*) and Chaos Engineering Experiments (*https://principlesofchaos.org*), in which you create controlled incidents on your schedule precisely to learn from them.

report and *distribute* (make the findings visible, shared). In your case, you will be sharing the impacts of your digitalization experiments, emphasizing the conditions necessary for people to engage fully with the process.[7]

The goal of your experiments is to gain insights into the ROI and other impacts of your changes. The same goals are needed from a good incident investigation process. Learning is the key to a successful digitalization rollout.

Continuously Reevaluating Your Strategy and Roadmap

The collection of experiments that make up your digitalization strategy and the order in which you explore them together are your roadmap. Each of your experiments ideally should be applied and learned from as rapidly as possible. You'll apply your changes to then evaluate whether you are getting signals that your target ROI is emerging.

This approach is essentially a tailoring of the scientific method as explained by the late, great Richard Feynman,[8] as shown in Figure 5-6.

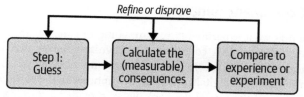

Figure 5-6. Richard Feynman's explanation of how the scientific method works

Using a similar approach, you can form a set of hypotheses using the various options under consideration, doctrine, and your own ideas to construct experiments that help you learn if the changes you are introducing to your value chains are gaining the ROI that your strategy was aiming for, as shown in Figure 5-7.

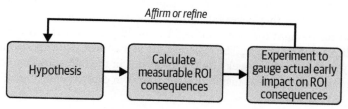

Figure 5-7. Due to the potentially complex nature of your value chains, your digitalization strategy will be constructed through a set of experiments that help you gradually explore the ROI on a set of measures you will implement

---

7 These conditions include psychological safety, avoiding simplistic root cause thinking, and avoiding blame.

8 Richard Feynman (*https://oreil.ly/UK1JT*) explains how the scientific method works.

A concrete example, shown in Figure 5-8, involves introducing a multicloud approach to a particular subset of a value chain to gain a measurable improvement in resiliency (i.e., ability to function under difficult conditions).

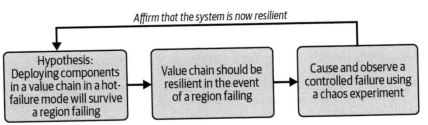

Figure 5-8. By investing in a value chain's resilience, given the hypothesis that enabling components of a value chain can be deployed in a hot-failure mode, you will be able to prove that the value chain can indeed survive conditions of region failure

Introducing Experiment Templates

The next question is what experiments *you* are going to consider for your digitalization roadmap. Strategic *doctrine* is a collection of recognized moves that you can make reach your strategic goal. Because you seek to learn and adapt as you move toward your target ROI, your doctrine for digitalization can be captured in the form of *experiment templates*. In each section of the rest of the book, we've provided a starter kit of experiments that we've applied to explore and gain digitalization ROI.

Note

Additional experiment templates for Chapters 7 and 8 are available for download at *https://oreil.ly/dfsac_experiments*.

The experiment templates are not comprehensive takes on the tool, technique, technology, or practice that they cover but more a solid starting point. The aim is to provide enough food for thought that you can begin to build your own experiments to advance your own digitalization efforts. The experiments you choose will depend entirely on the target ROI your organization seeks, so the templates in the following chapters serve only as a foundation you can use as inspiration for your own experimental digitalization steps.

6

Architecture and Governance

The success of your cloud digitalization strategy hinges on the decisions you make about how to create and evolve your value chains through technology. Crucial to your results are the changes you will make to the large-scale software system structures that support and enable your value chains. That structure is the *software architecture*.

Software architecture strives to answer just one question: What is the optimal organization and integration of technology that will support the needs of stakeholders and will survive the stresses placed upon it by those stakeholders. Distilled further: *What structure do we need to support and survive our stakeholders' needs and demands?*

Your digitalization strategy's success hinges on establishing, maintaining, and evolving this structure, this architecture, across all of your value chains, meeting all your diverse stakeholders' needs, while surviving the turbulence of different patterns of change and usage. No mean feat! It's no wonder that many try to avoid the question of architecture altogether and that people involved in defining architecture tend to be those with the most experience and seniority. The table stakes are just *that* high.

A helpful metaphor is to think of your system's architecture as a *habitat* (*https://oreil.ly/jSrnm*), that is, an environment or home within which your stakeholders reside. By viewing your systems as a habitat, you don't look at them as something merely used by your internal and external stakeholders. Instead, those important groups of people become part of the sociotechnical system—they populate it, they change with it,[1] they experience it, they are served by it (or not), they inhabit it.

How you evolve your architecture will affect each of those stakeholders, and each of those inhabitants will then stand in judgment on the delivered ROI of your digitalization strategy. They'll judge how well the sociotechnical system meets their needs, how well it supports them, and how great their experience is—or not—when interacting with your systems. Not all voices will be equal, but all will need to be heard in order for your digitalization to be a success.

---

1 Conway's law (*https://oreil.ly/d_KVB*) teaches us that "any organization that designs a system (defined broadly) will produce a design whose structure is a copy of the organization's communication structure."

Just like in nature, the laws governing this habitat are shaped by the ever-changing environment, in this case the market dynamics and the conditions of technology and stakeholder needs. It's crucial to strike a balance between managing risks posed by various scenarios and achieving a positive ROI. The architecture must be flexible and adaptable, able to accommodate changes while still providing essential support for stakeholders. Sustainable architecture decisions must take into account the mix of old and new requirements of the technology landscape.

An example of a habitat would be the collection of stakeholders and value chains that provide payments. The stakeholders of this capability could include:

Stakeholder	Description
Clients	The people who actually use the payment functionality.
Payment rail providers	The people who are instructed to settle the payments.
Product	The people who guide the development of payment through a collection of products the clients can use and maintain the relationships with the payment rail providers.
Engineering	The people who design, build, and perhaps even technically operate the solutions that meet the value chain's needs.
Technical operations	The people responsible for running the services, applications, platforms, etc. Could be the same people as the engineers if DevOps is an initiative.
Payment operations	The first line of resort for clients and payment rail providers when they have a query.
Anti-fraud	The people responsible for ensuring that payments obey sanctions and other restrictions.
Risk	The people responsible for assessing and governing the systems from a risk perspective (e.g., protection from fraud and money laundering, operational risk, etc.).
Finance	The people responsible for controlling the budgets and accounting for the work.
Upper management (executive committee)	The people responsible for knowing what the system does, what everyone is delivering, and how it dovetails beautifully, hopefully, with the organization's goals.

Stakeholders will be supported by one or more value chains that will, in turn, require your cloud architecture to support them. Taking a whole-system approach where the stakeholders and their experiences are part of the system (i.e., viewing your systems as a habitat) is essential to ensure you consider all these perspectives when prioritizing how to deliver your digitalization ROI. You may well decide that to deliver the best ROI, you need to leave existing systems as they are, maybe making some small changes to improve the engineers' experience, while pouring your digitalization into new value chains for new communities of stakeholders you want to bring in. Or you may decide on a strategy that balances your priorities across improvements to your existing value chains so they can scale to the heavens. Or, perhaps more likely, it will be a complicated and contentious mix of the two.

The tension, in this case, is desirable and important as it represents the natural balance between the different stakeholders' needs and your limited resources. As part of maximizing your ROI while executing your digitalization strategy, you will frequently need to manage and arbitrate the needs and experiences of your stakeholders as you decide on the valuable, small deliverables to roll out with your always-limited resources. By viewing your systems as a habitat, everyone gets a say as everyone stands to gain, or lose, from your efforts—even if only a few are actually picking up the cost and so have the loudest voices.

In this chapter, you will learn what to consider as you begin to evolve the value chains for your stakeholders to obtain your cloud digitalization ROI. Each consideration can be the basis for an experimental step on your path, to be used where you judge whether the trade-off of properties and ROI will be to your institution's advantage. We'll begin by exploring two of the key concepts you need to apply when assessing the architecture that already supports your existing value chains: modularity and cohesion.

Exploring the Structure That Supports, or Hinders, Your Value Chains

Architecture Says No

I'd lost patience, again. "Computer says no" pulsed through my head. Weary, I stared into the regretful eyes of my colleague and pleaded one last time, "Can we make this one small change?"

"Sorry, no, not right now," said my colleague. "The ESB will need to be updated, then join the manual testing cycle as part of the latest release train, only after being estimated and priced by our third-party supplier and approved by the enterprise architecture group, who are having their next meeting in a month. But our budget is set yearly, and this wasn't in it, so you will also need to run it by the chief technology officer to see if we can get it on the roadmap."

"But it's a small change!" I wept.

"Yes, yes, I know. But this is how we do things. It's a business-critical legacy system, provided off-the-shelf by our supplier, with dozens of different systems depending on it. Heck, even the bank depends on it. We can't just make a change ad hoc, or if we do, then you'll need to specify the change, the ESB will then need to be updated, then the manual testing..."

I tuned out. There was no one who could help me; the architecture was working against me. The architecture was saying no. It was Tuesday morning, and I was already begging for the weekend—the habitat had bitten back...

Although the story in the sidebar[2] took place in a financial services institution, it is a tragic tale in many technology-enabled business domains. In such circumstances, it is easy to blame one party or another, to rage at the organization, or even appeal to a higher power.[3] But only by revisiting your architecture can you stop one small change for one group from being an enormous and risky change for another, avoiding having one tiny amendment turn into a ripple of change that builds to a tsunami of swallowed budgets, delayed deliverables, and frustrated customers and executives.

It's stories like these that turn technology from an enabler into a hindrance. It's stories like these that your digitalization strategy will attempt to reduce. Doing better starts with figuring out what pieces of your value chains you should have so that your people can work on them, evolve them, and extend them in the ways your business and users need.

Everything starts with the architecture that you influence at the heart of your cloud digitalization strategy. In the habitat that is your systems and value chains, what application building blocks do you need, and what integration do you need to put them together? The architecture of your systems matters so much because it is the difference between supporting how your people need to work or frustrating your people's ability to get any work done.

The parts of your value chains, the structure within them, and the dependencies between those parts are your organization's technology habitat. The goal of great architecture in a financial services organization is nothing less than establishing a safe, secure, resilient, and reliable habitat—a habitat that serves the different ways that your people need and want to work in the face of a multitude of stressors and threats to the habitat, often unknown to you in advance. The challenge, and the stakes, couldn't be higher.

But before you can decide on the materials for your application building blocks and integrations and trade-offs between them, you need to explore the logical shape of these fundamental parts through the lens of your envisioned cloud architecture. What logical pieces do you need to enable your people to work effectively and deliver on your ROI? Answering that question starts with understanding the importance of the logical shape and properties of your system parts—it starts with modularity and cohesion.

Modularity and Cohesion Matter

Finding the right mix of components and their dependencies is critical to striking the right balance so your value chains can deliver your cloud digitalization strategy's ROI. You explore this decision using the joint tools of modularity and cohesion.

Modularity is an interesting term meaning "small measure." A module is something that can be measured, recognized separately, and put together with other modules within your system. In this way, the modularity you explore will not only be the modules that

---

2 If you're on pins and needles looking for some sort of resolution to this story, we will be revisiting it later in this chapter.

3 The finance department perhaps.

are the components of your value chains but also the modules that best serve you inside your components.[4]

Modularity is a powerful lens to view your architecture through, encouraging you to ask the question "Is this a 'good' module?" *Good* in this case means the module is a recognizable, standalone, defined piece of your system that you can think about in terms of how well it supports your value chains and how your people work. Modules are your building blocks, the bricks, that are the smallest measurable and evolving pieces of your architecture that are meaningful when assessed in isolation from one another as well as together in your value chains.

Note

A very typical example of a module in many financial services systems is the software service. A *service* is a runtime piece of your system that is independently executable, isolatable, and evolvable from other services and participates in your value chains either inside a value chain's component or by manifesting as the entire component.

When you have a good enough set of modules, change to the value chain is commensurate with what you expect. A small change tends to be, well, a small change, and therefore when you see a change play out across your modules, the ripple of subsequent changes doesn't surprise you too much.

Constantly asking yourself what change your evolving architecture supports through your digitalization transformation is a key way to verify if your modularity is improving or degrading your system's ability to handle the pace and type of change you can anticipate. In addition to exploring how commensurately your modularity supports the stresses of change, you can also verify at design and runtime how your modularity handles other stresses, such as tolerance of failure, updates, and ongoing maintenance, and ultimately how it delivers your digitalization's ROI.

The impact, frequency, and speed with which your components and value chains can embrace change are principally enabled or resisted by the side effects of that change, and modularity is your key tool in helping to reduce those side effects such as those in the story I started the previous section with. Get your modularity good enough, and change and its side effects become reasonable and embraceable at the speed of change your system requires. Get it wrong, and everything becomes difficult.

The example given in "Exploring the Structure That Supports, or Hinders, Your Value Chains" on page 43 walks through the type of collaboration that results (i.e., a painful one) when modularity works against you. A single change results in a ripple of change side effects across the system. When you have the wrong modules, with too many tight dependencies, maintained in vastly different ways and evolved at entirely different speeds, a small change quickly escalates into six months of work.

---

4 For the Latin geeks, *component* comes from the Latin for "putting together," the verb *componere*, itself composed from *com-* ("together") and *ponere* ("put").

When you have a poor approach to modularity and integration, every change runs the risk of instigating a maelstrom of burdensome, expensive, and distracting changes. Every change has an impact, a blast radius, that far outreaches the scope of the original change, and as these changes mount up your systems, they become the reasons you cannot seize the business opportunities that come your way, rather than being the reason you can. Your systems become the inertia, not the enabler. Your systems become your legacy, which is not a good thing in software engineering, as it usually means those are the systems that are hard to change. They might be making you money, but they are also the inertia that means you can't seize the next opportunity.

Legacy and the Friction of Change

One key reason that systems and components are declared to be "legacy" and rewritten is that the architecture they manifest, specifically the modularity of that architecture, is now so painfully in conflict with the change needed by the business that every change becomes big and painful.

No architecture is entirely future-proof, but by investing in the modularity of and careful dependencies between your systems throughout your digitalization journey, you can optimize for flexibility, extensibility, and adaptability and contribute to a longer active, value-adding life for your system as a whole.

When you take the time to consider stresses like change across your modules as you plan your architectural changes, you can even bake in the potential to re-architect, remove, even retire modules in your system when new business pressures come to light. Modularity is a key tool you can use, alongside coupling, to help you *architect for replaceability* and even for unforeseen stresses in the future.

Your digitalization strategy has the need and opportunity to revisit your architecture's modularity. Key deliverables on your strategy will focus on improving your system's modularity, but toward what end? What does good modularity look and feel like? How will you know it when you've got it?

WHAT DOES GOOD MODULARITY LOOK AND FEEL LIKE?

A module is a *unit of change* in your architecture. Get a module right, and change can be embraced; get it wrong, and change is resisted. There are three properties that you will look to enable during your digitalization strategy's architectural changes to deliver modules that can serve your organization best. You will aim for modules that are highly cohesive, composable, and loosely coupled.

A module as one reason to change and one job to do: High cohesion

A module's first and most important job is to be able to evolve according to the speed and pressures required of it. A good module starts by having a set of contents that can and do change together, naturally. Grouping things together that change together in a module is the first test of whether or not you have the right modules.

Grouping things together that change together often leads to the second test of a good module: Does it have a single job to do? A module that does too much will have to change for a myriad of unrelated reasons, leading to change friction. This quality is often referred to as *cohesion*. A highly cohesive module does one thing and does it well.

Making your modules focused and cohesive also pays dividends for your engineers. The biggest limiting factor in being able to confidently change a module is human comprehension. If your people cannot comprehend a module because it is doing a dozen different complicated things, then even with good testing, it is going to be slower to evolve as they have to learn and relearn how to navigate the entangled contents of the module every time it needs to change. Getting the right modules can encourage simpler (i.e., disentangled) code as the modules will gravitate toward having only one job to do each—one job, one reason to change, and minimal side effects from entanglement.

These benefits are why re-architecting toward more cohesive modules is such a powerful tool in helping your architecture support the ROI of the digitalization of your value chains. Keeping a module focused on the one thing it needs to do, and only that thing, by extracting those other, unrelated jobs to other modules is a very common deliverable on a digitalization strategy's backlog.

Highly Cohesive Modules in Action for the Past 50+ Years: UNIX Command-Line Tools

A great example of the longevity of a set of highly cohesive and loosely coupled modules is Unix command-line tools. Unix command-line tools follow the "pipe and filter" architectural approach, where every tool does one job and is easily composable into complicated systems by "piping" the output of one tool to the input of another.

The pipe and filter–style architecture has become very popular in modern financial systems, although rather than simple command-line tools being the "filters," or processors, and Unix pipes transporting data between the tools, you will find simple independent processes or services that can be composed through network interfaces, such as HTTP, REST, etc.

This focus on small, single-purpose and composable service-oriented architectures is the key difference between microservices and more monolithic services. Microservices architectures are composed of simple, single-job services that can be flexibly, even dynamically, composed into new pipelines to meet the needs of a new or fast-changing value chain.

Composable

Changing architectural decisions is often hard. It is supposed to be. If you have collection of modules that need a large number of other services to do their jobs, an that need to be evolved in lockstep with those other modules for things to work, the changing the mix of those modules is going to be so hard that you'd only ever consider as a big-ticket investment (i.e., part of your digitalization strategy). But it doesn't have t be that way, if you consider the composability and coupling between your services.

A module is composable if it is easy to understand, use, or replace without havin to disentangle it from dozens of other modules. If the module has a single, obvious jo to do, that can be instigated in a single, focused way, and if it has as few dependencie as possible, it is ready to be composed into existing and new value chains. By having small surface area (one job), revealing its intended use (a simple, focused way of usin it), and having minimal dependencies (and useful documentation), your modules wi actively *encourage* your people to compose modules selected from the standard base set c defined modules into whatever pipelines and value chains you require. A module that i composable is a joy to architect and use.

Loosely coupled

It's no use having a module that is ripe for reuse and composition into new valu chains if it is glued to the services that use it and depend upon it. For a module to b composable, it needs to be repurposable easily into new value chains, and that mean it needs to be loosely tied to everything it interacts with and everything that interact with it.

It can be helpful to think of everything a module interacts with as being a *contrac* To give your module as much flexibility as possible, you look to design the contract suc that if either side of the contractual arrangement needs to evolve, the other side doesn' need to be told.

This requires the contract between the modules to be designed such that th internals of neither side of the relationship are accidentally leaked into the contract otherwise, an internal change will cause an external change, and we're back to thos frustrating, delay-inducing ripples again. You also may choose to make the contrac flexible enough that there's plenty of room for either side to change what they send o receive from one another by making the sender as strict as possible but the receiver a open and flexible as they can be.[5]

If two modules are too closely coupled (i.e., strongly glued together) for their needs you will experience architectural pain like that in the conversation we shared at th beginning of this chapter.

Carefully considering how to loosen the contracts between your modules and th environment they rely on—making them as loose and interchangeable as they need t be—is one of the goals of the investments you'll be making as part of your digitalizatio strategy if speed of change is one of your target ROIs.

---

5 The "Robustness Principle" (*https://oreil.ly/8_BkY*) is one example of how this can be encouraged.

MODULES IN ACTION: SERVICES, APPLICATIONS, BOUNDED CONTEXTS, AND PLATFORMS

If modules and coupling are your hammer and chisel when exploring what you may evolve in your value streams for your digitalization strategy, then bounded contexts and services are your marble. You'll work from the smallest module (the service) through to collections of services or monoliths that evolve loosely together (bounded contexts) until you achieve self-service, cross-value-chain-cutting capabilities.

Independent, autonomous, single-job services

Services are the smallest material in your architecture. To be a service, the module needs to be independently evolvable and thus take into account all of the guidelines for a good module and coupling.

A service should also be autonomous, in that it is constructed, built, executed, and retired independently. To maximize comprehensibility and ease of management by the people who build and operate the service, aiming for it doing one, specific, job in your value chains is again important to make your service a good module. Fine-grained or coarse-grained; strong or loosely coupled. Granularity and glue.

Since a service is the smallest unit of modularity in your architecture—not necessarily your internal software *design*—it's also useful to think of a service as being your smallest unit of *optionality* (i.e., the smallest unit where you can vary your choice of properties). Because your services are independent and autonomous, they also represent a unit that can be independently scaled, made resilient to failure, secured, maintained, etc. Each of the desirable properties you might want can be explored, at the micro level, and optimized for each of your services. Your services are your smallest levers to move the world that is your value chain toward your digitalization ROI.

Libraries, Frameworks, and More?

Libraries, frameworks, packages, classes, and functions are all crucial tools for code-level modularity. When you design your services, be they whole applications or small, single-function microservices, good coding practice encourages identifying modules at this level to help the codebase be navigable, comprehensible, and evolvable.

While these types of module implementation are critical to the engineering experience of working with your codebases, it is services, applications, bounded contexts, and platforms that are the primarily architectural-level implementations of modularity.

Applications, APIs, and bounded contexts

Applications and APIs are logical collections of functionality, often collected to suit a particular group of users. The key difference is that an application is built to be consumed by groups of people, whereas an API is targeted for consumption by other machines.

Applications and APIs can be as small as a single tool that does one job or as broad as an entire payments ecosystem. At the smallest level, the line between what is an application and what is a service is blurry enough to not be too important. Both small applications and services, each perhaps presenting small, focused APIs, aim to be independent and autonomous and do their one job well.

At the other end of the scale, applications could be composed of a large set of functions—what is often labeled a "monolithic" application, such as a core banking system—where all of the functions can be impacted by change to the application. This is often the case where a part of a value chain has been acquired as a third-party application. The main limitation here is that the whole application is evolved together and so if different functions have different speeds of change, different reliability or resilience needs, or different optionality needs, then building and managing everything together can slow the overall speed of change.

Bounded contexts are groupings of multiple services and applications that are physically demarcated because different groups of people who *do not often work together* are responsible for each group. A bounded context can be optimized to support close collaboration among the people, even teams of people, who will work on that area of your value chains.

The types of concepts that people in a bounded context use, the language they use to describe their systems, will be the same (i.e., domain specific), and supporting a common language helps these teams work fast within the boundary. Anti-corruption layers (ACLs) are software structures whose sole job is to translate the domain language used in one bounded context to another bounded context. An ACL will translate between the domain language used by the different groups of people so no one has to create centralized, brittle, canonical domain language for the entire value chain or organization.

A *bounded context* is a collaborative way of working in an organization; see more in Chapter 7, "People, Process, and Organizational Structure". For this reason, it is almost the largest recognizable structure in your architecture that can be identified as a module at all, according to the rules of what makes a good module. That is, except for platforms.

Platforms

Platforms are collections of services, applications, tooling, APIs, and even bounded contexts that provide common, often self-service, functions to multiple, often all, value streams. A platform brings together a set of independently evolving functions into a cohesive whole that can be depended on across your whole architecture.

When you need to establish common, consistently managed and evolved sets of functionality that can be reused across multiple value chains, you have the opportunity for a platform. You have to be careful not to cause too much friction between the different rates of change across the platform's functions to optimize the maneuverability required by market and business changes. This is often done by decomposing a platform internally into bounded contexts, applications, and services. Platforms are a great option when you want to serve several value streams across your organization with a single consistent capability. Good examples are self-service application platforms-as-a-service (PaaS) such as Red Hat OpenShift.

Architectural Styles in Financial Services

When you examine your current architecture and how it serves your value chains and stakeholders, you will likely identify a multitude of different architectural styles. Architectural styles are like most fashions—what was last year's hottest number is today's three-quarter-length trousers. Expensive, ugly, and more than a little disappointing, to be hidden away in favor of the new fashion.

Chances are very good that your current architecture is a mishmash of yesterday's styles and tomorrow's legacy, and that's OK. No matter the breakdown of your components, systems, and services across your value streams, if those streams can evolve as fast as you need them to, and you're getting the ROI you seek from them, don't swap those timeless little black dresses for today's trendiest option just because all the cool organizations are doing it (or are pretending to do it). Your digitalization strategy can be smarter than that; you can establish your mix of timeless, vintage, and haute couture but avoid becoming an (architectural) fashion faux pas.

You probably can identify a mix of the following styles:

- Layered

- Pipeline

- Microkernel

- Service-based

- Event-driven

- Orchestration-driven

- Microservices

The list does go on, and none of these styles are *bad*. They just present different trade-offs of advantages and disadvantages,[6] and many are children of their times. Truth is that most systems end up a mix of services, fine and coarse grained, with some large, often third-party, monoliths for nondifferentiating stuff (rapidly moving to being SaaS products) and a couple of platforms to support some key ways of working internally.

There are exceptions. There's a mainframe in Switzerland that's still resisting attempts to be retired (and succeeding in keeping the COBOL contracts market alive) or you might have a core banking system or platform so entangled with every other system that it represents an un-upgradable, unreplaceable ball of Christmas tree lights. Of course, these aren't good things, but they aren't entirely bad unless they are holding

---

6 To help you identify and explore the advantages and disadvantages of these different styles, we recommend the deep dive captured in *Fundamentals of Software Architecture: An Engineering Approach* by Mark Richards and Neal Ford (O'Reilly).

your business back. They probably are, but you never know—not until you explore them through the tools of modularity and residuality,[7] employing your digitalization ROI.

Evolving Architecture: The "Impossible" Job

How do you know whether your architectural styles are serving you? How do you explore what different style, different modularity might better support your value chains and the needs of your stakeholders? How do you decide what valuable deliverables to build to evolve your architecture and improve your habitat? How do you explore not only what could be better today but what needs to be better for tomorrow?

And just to up the ante, these architectural decisions are not only your biggest lever but also your biggest risk. You simply cannot afford to get these things wrong.

This is why architecture is often reduced to meaningless "PowerPoint fiction," or vacuous following of the latest fashionable architectural style. Architecture is *hard* because it exists to evolve a complex system, the habitat itself, in order to get the ROI for your digitalization. There is no architectural style recipe that is the silver bullet for now and always.

This is why being the architect, being the person or group that has to make these calls, is the "impossible job." You are navigating a complex space, so you know you need to probe, sense, and respond, but what does better even look like? You know what ROI you want, but how do you turn that into the right change when there isn't a silver bullet on a consultant's PowerPoint slide?

Modularity is your scalpel, but where should you make your incisions? How do you make the big calls? Is it really an impossible dilemma? Up until recently, your only resort was to copy other companies, get a gut feeling from people you hope had the right guts, or trust to luck—but not anymore. You now have *residuality*.

The answer to "What should we invest in and change architecturally?" starts not with the question of what modularity you need to make things work—that's usually the easy answer and as far as most PowerPoint decks go. Residuality is a different way of thinking about and planning your architectural investments. It starts not with how things will work or how you will get your ROI but instead with how they, and you, won't.

RESIDUALITY STARTS WITH THE NAIVE

Does the architectural hypothesis perform the needed functionality for the value chain? This question is perhaps obvious when discussing an existing value chain, but it can still prompt some work to be done if an existing value chain needs to be evolved to a new purpose or a whole new value chain needs to be created.

Most architectural work begins and ends with answering this question. As soon as the structure seems reasonable enough to support the functionality needed, it's time to move on. Perhaps some great architects might pause to ask a few awkward questions

---

7 According to Barry M. O'Reilly (*https://oreil.ly/_GeOA*), "residuality theory provides a basis for designing software systems with resilient and antifragile behavior through understanding sensitivity to stress and the concept of residual behaviors."

around whether a database is being relied on by too many services, or whether reusing an existing service is a good idea or not this time around, but mainly the work is done with the answer to "Does the structure support the functionality for the stakeholders?"

But when you think in terms of residuality, how the structure will work to support the necessary business functionality is only the *first* step. A hint as to what is missing is likely in the digitalization ROI that you're aiming for. This initial hypothesis for what could be a candidate architecture might satisfy the ROI of the value chain's functionality, but does it deliver scalability, security, and resilience?

This first hypothesis for your architecture is called the *naive architecture*. It's only been subjected to the test of meeting stakeholder needs for functionality. If you stop there, and many do, you may achieve that ROI, but only under naive circumstances. As soon as such an architecture encounters change, or real-world conditions, it is unlikely to fare well.

WHAT SURVIVES?

With naive architecture in hand, the next step is to explore what of this architecture survives (i.e., still functions) under the turbulent stressors of the real world. This is where you can start to build confidence that your architecture will deliver on your ROI. How will your architecture respond to various forms of change? How will your architecture survive under changes in load? How will thunder lizards on the beaches of Amsterdam affect your architecture?[8]

Through carefully considering a list of expected and surprising circumstances that your architecture may or, counterintuitively, may not encounter, you develop a number of *residual* architectures. Each one represents more and more of what survives, the *residues*, under these different circumstances. You can compare how well they each meet the ROI you're seeking for your digitalization strategy.

What this approach does is give you a way to explore, before making some expensive decisions, the ROI of your big and small architectural decisions and deliverables for your digitalization backlog. Through the lens of each possibility's ROI, you can look at the development of each hypothetical architecture and examine how it fares under your realistic, and unrealistic, stressors until eventually you believe you have explored enough.

THERE CAN BE ONLY ONE: WHAT SURVIVES, WINS

You don't need to spend hours dreaming up stressors and adjusting your architectural hypotheses to get huge value out of this exercise. Hundreds of different stressors are not required even for complicated financial systems; tens of stressors are enough for you to start to see that hypothetical architectures able to survive one stressor are often well suited to survive another. At that point, you're ready to decide that you have done the

---

8 There's a (scientific) method to this madness. Residuality theory explains that by exploring the wildest of cases, you are gravitating toward an architecture that is better prepared for the unknown unknowns it is likely to encounter. It's also fun. See Barry O'Reilly's "The Philosophy of Residuality Theory" (*https://oreil.ly/ p2SBt*) and "Residuality Theory" (*https://oreil.ly/IfE8f*).

impossible: you've found an architecture that can survive many circumstances, even the unforeseen, and that you are more confident will actually deliver on your desired ROI.

Residuality and Regulations

A change in banking regulations (e.g., the introduction of the Digital Operational Resilience Act [DORA] (*https://oreil.ly/PC4yD*) in the European Union) can mean wholescale panic for your company and often has a myriad of impacts on your value chains. Rarely is an amendment to regulations limited to peripheral concerns, and we all know that penalties for nonconformance can be severe, even including legal consequences.

For this reason, it's important to include regulatory changes as potential stressors when exploring the residuality of your planned structure and value chains. By looking at your architectural plans through the lens of regulatory churn early, and then often as your governance continuously evolves, you can turn your reasonable fears into an architectural advantage.

By exploring your residual architectures, you can combine the best characteristics of each into your final architecture. This final hypothesis is the one that gives you the best chance of survival under all the stressors, realistic and not, that you considered, and it can be thought of as the "informed" architecture. You're now in a place to plot a course toward your informed architecture, capturing each valuable step as a deliverable in your digitalization backlog with more confidence than many before you.

If the naive architecture was like a child leaving the sheltered environs of their school or college, the informed architecture is the mature adult who has the scars and has built up the immune system to survive most of life's travails. We know which architecture we'd prefer to rely on for our ROI.

Governing the Ungovernable

It's one thing to set the stage for ROI-driven architectural changes, encouraged by exploring what survives through residuals. It's quite another to turn those plans into action and keep to your best path as your journey progresses. When each step is an experiment in finding your ROI, architectural governance changes from being an exercise conducted by the anointed few to being a continual stream of guidance from education through guardrails to policing.

If architecture is the impossible job, architectural governance is the art of the ungovernable. In a healthy, innovative digitalization environment, all things will be challenged in the light of your architectural experiments. In the course of seeking your digitalization ROI, you will make missteps and some of your ideas and choices will be wrong. An approach to governance needs to embrace how wrong you are regularly going to be rather than be a fake safety net of inappropriate assurances.

Things seemed so easy when you were simply digitizing work processes. Copying and pasting from analog, manual, human labor–intensive work to digital technologies required little innovation. You could establish the principles, set the guidelines, gather the education, set up the regular reviews and audits, pick your favorite architectural style, and go! The only thing to learn was *how* to bring those processes from the mechanical to the digital; little innovative thought was required.

Digitalization requires reinvention; it requires innovation. It requires crafting the new processes and value chains that are now possible with the advent of cloud technologies. The game hasn't just been changed; it is being reinvented. Digitalization is disruptive, so your architecture will be disruptive as well. All is up for change, and as your architectural strategy adapts, so will the governance needed to guide it.

You will still need to consider your guiding architectural principles, gather the necessary education, and arrange the many workshops and reviews needed before and after each experimental step. But those principles, that education, those guardrails and policies themselves will be up for examination as new information comes to light.

And that's not all. Even as you concoct your best-laid plans for automated policies, education, guidance, audits, and reviews, you may well encounter the disturbing fact that your hard work is hindering rather than helping your architecture evolve. You may find that in this new world of constant innovation, your governance struggles to keep up. Worse, it may even be ignored.

THE PARABLE OF THE IGNORED (CLOUD) ARCHITECTS

Being ignored was exactly the condition in one digitalization strategy in a traditional financial services institution, and we cloud architects[9] were despairing. Being a passionate lot, we had explored the many adjustments we could make to our value chains and the underpinning architectures to make the most of the flexible, adaptable cloud resources that we were planning. Our target ROI was simple: increase the delivery frequency—agility and speed—and performance of the value chain such that new applications can be created in weeks, not months, to open up dozens of new clients and markets.

Initially there was some success. Remember the story of woe from "Exploring the Structure That Supports, or Hinders, Your Value Chains" on page 43? Where one small change resulted in weeks of delays because of poor modularity, separation of concerns, and centralization?

Now, the centralized approach that was a combination of enterprise service bus and one-database-to-rule-them-all was no more. When the ripples of change and results of stress were examined through the lens of residuality, the current solution stood out like a sore thumb for being a brittle entanglement of concerns-in-a-box. Rather than reducing the complexity of the system's interconnections, the solution had resulted in a hideous,

---

9 Recently rebranded from "enterprise architects," with a healthy salary bump of course.

unmaintainable mess of untested, untestable smart pipes,[10] maintained by exasperate
engineers fighting poorly written user interfaces.

Under the examination of residuality it became painfully obvious that the curren
solution had to go. But reducing the role of the centralized ESB (enterprise service bus
and database turned out to be the easy step, exploring what replaced it was where th
tough questions arose. There was the potential for chaos. All those reliability and securit
concerns that had been helpfully wrapped up in an ESB- and database-shaped box migh
have meant a rat's nest of productivity- and speed-of-change-sapping entanglement, bu
now those concerns were pushed to the people creating the services themselves. Hov
would best practices be encouraged if they couldn't be centralized?

Worse than that, every enterprise architect knows what the default response to a
enterprise architect is by an engineering team. They're ignored. Politely perhaps, bu
generally ignored. We knew that too. We knew we had good ideas, important guidance
crucial educational materials, to help the teams re-architect and run their services on th
cloud, but also that there was every chance that we'd be completely, and utterly, ignored
As the architecture decentralized to support the necessary ROI, so the job of governin
the architecture became impossible. Chaos ruled.

And so chaos became a key part of our answer.

MAKING THE ARCHITECTURE UNIGNORABLE BY MAKING PRODUCTION UNIGNORABLE

Residuality helps you consider the real world when exploring what architecture you wan
to employ *before* you build it. But residuality is easy to ignore when your engineerin
teams are in the heat of a sprint and looking to produce the new solution as quickly a
possible. This is where governance is supposed to come into play—when ideas turn t
action.

But governance fails when it is a quiet voice in the background reminding people t
do the right thing. Governance also fails when it becomes the authoritarian ruler, leavin
no room for innovative thinking. One approach results in ignorance; the other resistance
even riot.

There is a third path: make your residuality thinking a *dynamic* presence as you
architectural hypotheses are brought to life. As you take each step toward attemptin
to improve your architecture, you can verify your returns straight away *and* use that t
encourage an interest in your governance. You can make your engineering teams hungr
for the principles, guidance, education, and safety guardrails of your governance. All yo
need is to introduce a little stress, a little *chaos.*

GOVERNANCE: PROACTIVE, CONTINUOUS, CHAOS ENGINEERING

Rather than taking a back seat, governance in a lively digitalization transformatio
becomes a proactive practice. It begins with the usual suspects: deciding on the guidin
principles, policies, and education that you think will support the architectural adjust
ments you plan to make to unlock your target ROI.

---

10 James Lewis and Martin Fowler, "Microservices" (*https://oreil.ly/ScRN6*).

Then, instead of sitting back and waiting for the engineers to volunteer for your wisdom, you make the conditions of production, the conditions of the real world, present under your control. You inject the turbulence, the stress, that makes your governance desirable, even needed, by your teams. You codify the stressors you subjected your architecture to when exploring your residual architectures so that they deliberately, and ideally safely, subject the work of the engineering teams to those same stressors through a series of frequent, controlled *experiments*.

Each experiment is a reminder and a proof of what was needed. Do the hypotheses of the original architectural decisions hold up in reality? Are we surprised by how the architecture responds? Do we even need to change the architecture if it survives when we thought it might fail? These experiments don't even have to be a surprise! Everyone can know about and be a part of codifying and running these experiments, and then, if they fail, it is to your architectural governance that your teams will look.

Everything from the security of your architecture, its resulting reliability, through to its resilience to failure can be explored *for real*. Each time the implementation fails, it is from the architectural governance that advice will be sought. What principles could help? What guardrails could be applied to make things safer? What better observability do we need? What cloud features could we take advantage of?

This is not a hypothetical story. This is how an enabling platform for chaos engineering was adopted by a bank. You can imagine the reaction that a bank might have to the notion of adopting *chaos* engineering. "We saw 2008, and not again thank-you-very-much!"

But when this approach was presented as a way to obtain speed of delivery and high-performance systems—proveably, securely, and reliably—while taking full advantage of cloud computing...demonstrably delivering the sought-after ROI of digitalization? "Yes, please" was the answer we got instead.

Proactive, continuous governance through chaos engineering experiments, backed up by a healthy cadre of principles, guardrails, and education makes your architecture, and the residuality that informed it, unignorable. We might have ended up calling it "Continuous Governance through Controlled, Limited Scope Disaster Recovery Experiments" to the rest of the bank, but at its heart, it was chaos engineering, and its value did not stop at just making the architects, architecture, and the governance unignorable. There was one last treat in store.

EVOLVING GOVERNANCE

Through the combination of residuality and chaos engineering—albeit perhaps rebranded as "Continuous Governance Through Controlled, Limited Scope Disaster Recovery" for consumption in a financial services organization—we generated a hunger and a need for what governance could supply. One problem, however, persisted: we didn't have all the answers. Our governance was evolving as our architectural ideas for unlocking our ROI hit reality. We were going to lack answers; we were going to be caught out.

Then a small miracle happened. A team did indeed find a condition that our governance could not offer advice on. So the *team* proposed a new approach. A one-off. An outlier. Just an idea.

It was a brilliant idea. We added the idea to our governance package. We created a new set of education around it, some best practices, even a library implementation for reuse. Our governance had grown *because* of the work our teams were doing. We didn't need to be the experts; our teams had become willing and passionate contributors to the architectural governance itself. They created their own experiments to explore real-world residuality, and now they had come up with a new, repeatable way of embracing that turbulence to make our systems resilient in a whole host of new circumstances.

And then it happened again. And again. And it never stopped.

We'd stumbled on a way not only of making architectural governance unignorable but also of ensuring that it evolved collaboratively across the organization. As our architecture evolved to unlock our digitalization's ROI, so did our architectural governance and, best of all, we didn't have to be the gurus, gatekeepers, and police of that governance. We became simply the curators of a healthy feedback loop, a community of like-minded professionals that we'd established, ready for future digitalization efforts as we unlocked more and more ROI through informed architectures and continually, proactively applied, and evolving governance.

Architecture and Governance Experiment Templates

The scope and impact of your architecture, and how it can help or hinder the performance and evolution of your habitat's value chains, leads to many different experiments you could consider to unlock your digitalization ROI. The following is a small sample of the ones we have seen have the most impact.

EXPERIMENT TEMPLATE: CLOUD VARIANTS

All cloud types aim to deliver on-demand, self-service allocation and management of elastic compute and data resources. Whether you're trying to run an immense monolithic application or the latest and greatest tiny function of code, whether you have a small relational database or are planning a data mesh, your cloud platform, or mixture of cloud platforms, will likely have you covered.

The key differences between cloud strategies are flexibility of scale, underlying cost model, and, arguably, security attack surfaces. The key ones to consider as part of this experiment are:

Private clouds

A uniform experience is the goal here. If the cloud inside your organization looks and behaves the same as someone else's cloud, then you have the means to leverage your existing investment in compute and storage resources while enabling the same speed and flexibility that is expected of a self-serve cloud—within the constraints of what you have available of course. If it's your data center, it's your limitation on scale.

It's also a stable expenditure. Your data center costs what it costs, and it is a shared cost across everyone who uses it as it always has been. This can make it complicated to experiment with FinOps, but it does mean that accounting can largely apply the same approach that it has in the past.

Public clouds

Public clouds[11] are all about giving you the sense of infinite scale. Value-add services are also a differentiator, as older infrastructure services become heavily commoditized and undifferentiated.

Cost is as flexible as your public cloud's scale and about a hundred times as complicated. Tracking and controlling costs can be a considerable challenge, one beginning to be addressed by the FinOps approach.

Multicloud

It's not one cloud to rule them all. Using more than a single public cloud is very common. For example, you might use one provider's cloud for end-user computing (e.g., Microsoft 365 & Azure), another provider's cloud for applications and databases (e.g., AWS or GCP), and some specialized clouds with software as a service (e.g., Salesforce, Workday, Service Now).

Hybrid clouds

A mixture of private and public clouds is very common in financial services, with some legacy assets residing on more custom internal clouds and newer value chains being built directly for the cloud using cloud native approaches.

What's the difference between *multicloud* and *hybrid cloud?*
Interoperability between multiple public clouds, between public and private clouds, and portability of applications between these computing environments are important requirements to be successful with hybrid cloud.

Picking the right cloud for your value chains is going to require a careful analysis of cost, scale, and how you can leverage your existing investment. Building in a cloud-native way, discussed next, helps you avoid vendor lock-in and be ready to move workloads across the different cloud options open to you. A mixture of approaches, even a multi-cloud approach, is very likely, unless you are a FinTech start-up or scale-up.

Cloud variant ROI signals

In this case, any and all of your target digitalization ROI can frame your decisions for this experiment and can be the source of the signals you detect as you evolve your value chains toward the different cloud variants. There's no one signal that's more important or evident than the others. You'll be looking for them all.[12]

.1 The term *public cloud* is often used to mean the large clouds of the "hyperscalers": Amazon Web Services, Microsoft Azure, Google Cloud Platform, etc.

2 All the ones important to you.

Cloud variant caveats

Always ask yourself, "Am I gaining real ROI by moving a value chain, or system component, to the cloud?" This sounds like a ridiculously obvious question, but it's an important consideration that we've seen ignored countless times.

Moving a workload to gain the advantages of one cloud or another always involves effort, so you must make sure the decision is backed by hard ROI signals that you can see being delivered by the target cloud mix you are moving to. Otherwise, as we mentioned in Chapter 1, "moving to the cloud" has the same potential for disappointment as "digitizing our processes."

Example hypothesis

> *Evolving integrations to serverless in a public cloud will reduce risk and increase efficiency.*

A payment pipeline in a large financial services institution contained a mishmash of different adaptors to in-country payment systems. Working on these integrations was a headache, and running them was like trying to herd cats. The actual code in these integrations was relatively small, even tiny, but the work involved in building, packaging, and deploying them along with the rest of a monolith increased risk unacceptably. Also, if one integration failed, so did the rest of the system.

Decoupling these integrations and running them as discrete, event-driven functions on a public cloud reduced the complexity of the components, increased their resilience to failure, and allowed us to scale these components independently from the rest of the application. This was important, as some rails were in much higher demand than others.

EXPERIMENT TEMPLATE: CLOUD NATIVE

Cloud native is that rare thing, a marketing buzzword with sound architectural foundations. The starting point for cloud native is the question, "What would your system look like if you actually architected, designed, and built to reside in the cloud from inception?" A cloud-native application is designed to reside in the cloud from the start. It involves cloud technologies like APIs, microservices, container orchestration, and auto-scaling.

Cloud native combines a multitude of technologies and architectural styles, and it encourages an approach to development and operations that focuses on enabling all the options you have when you target the cloud, whether that is a private cloud running in your data center, a public hyperscale cloud, or a clever combination of both. With cloud native, you architect, design, build, and run to take advantage of whatever mix of cloud makes the most sense for you.

Typically, cloud native encompasses the following technical considerations:

Microservices
> Break apart your value chains and system components into smaller services to promote more optionality around scale and reliability, as well as encouraging smaller packages of change and so lower risk deployments and reduced blast radius of failure (*https://oreil.ly/inpJC*).

Containers

Package your code and its dependencies in one versioned, easy to deploy, runnable unit.

Functions as a service (or serverless)

Provide an even more fine-grained unit of deployment and runtime capability, often deployed on a serverless platform that reduces the need for business-engineering teams to manage infrastructure resources.

API focus

Encourage APIs as the mature goal for inter- and intra-system communications, echoing team communication lines.

Service meshes

Extract complex orthogonal concerns from your service code and into the surrounding infrastructure of a mesh that works between the services. An example is moving tracing out of your services and into the links between services.

Autoscaling

Automatically scale up or down service instances (e.g., containers or serverless functions) in reaction to workload demand.

Design for operability and resilience

From the outset, design software components to be observed and managed in operations (see "Experiment Template: Surface Everything with Observability" on page 80 for more on this). Also, through patterns such as circuit breakers and bulkheads, introduce resiliency signals and levers to help your value chains, and chains of microservices, absorb challenging, sometimes unpredictable, conditions (see "Experiment Template: Engineer Resilience" on *https://oreil.ly/dfsac_experiments*).

Cloud native enables and encourages the following development approaches:

Continuous integration and continuous deployment

Enable applications and services to be integrated and delivered continuously (i.e., at any point in time) rather than waiting on a larger batch of changes; "Introducing Experiment Templates" on page 40 shows this experiment template used as an example.

DevOps, DevSecOps, and FinOps

Encourage close collaboration among development, operations, security, and even finance (see Chapter 7).

Enabling and encouraging a GitOps management approach with infrastructure as code (IaC), policy as code, etc.

Use of a central source code repository (mostly Git, thus the name GitOps) as the Source of Truth to describe the desired state of the computing environment. GitOps is an operational framework that applies DevOps best practices used

for application development (e.g., version control, collaboration, compliance, an
CI/CD) to infrastructure and platform automation.

Cloud-native ROI signals

Signals and stories you can expect to observe when applying cloud native approache
include (but are not limited to):

- Faster and less risky deployments
- Platform, and cloud, independence

Cloud-native caveats

Like many of the tools, techniques, and skills that come with making the most of th
cloud, building new systems the cloud-native way may well require your people to adop
new skills and thinking to get the full advantage of the approach. The ROI of convertin
existing systems to this approach may also be minimal, so you can consider the Wra
Legacy Platforms Experiment Template for those situations.

Example hypothesis

Fine-grained services lead to greater reliability in a payment rail.

One payment system to rule them all was a problem. Using cloud-native approaches
especially microservices and containers, we broke apart a payment pipeline into discret
payment pipelines for different rails and were able to independently scale and evolv
those rails to the unique requirements of the clients and destinations. The speed o
change of the system was increased from once a month to several times an hour, as eacl
release could be made independently between and inside each payment pipeline.

EXPERIMENT TEMPLATE: WRAP AND RETIRE LEGACY PLATFORMS WITH APIS

Sometimes the lift required to make a system runnable on the cloud just does not justif
any potential returns. A huge, Oracle forms–based behemoth of a monolith is going tc
gain very little from simply moving hosting from one location to another. All of the dial
available to you, even if you build your systems in a cloud-native way, will be stuck fo
these systems, so what can you do?

The best approach we've seen is to apply the API-driven approach of cloud native
combined with the anti-corruption patterns of domain-driven design,[13] to wrap you:
legacy systems in a facade that allows the rest of your value chains to evolve toward clouc
native. Then, when you decide you're ready,[14] you can choose to re-engineer or repurch
ase parts of the legacy complex subsystem *if* you see significant ROI in taking that systen
into the cloud. This is an application of the strangler-fig pattern (*https://oreil.ly/grtHO*)

---

13 See *Domain-Driven Design: Tackling Complexity in the Heart of Software* by Eric Evans.

14 Or the pain of the legacy system holding your ROI back just becomes too much.

and we've seen it work for peripheral parts of a value chain as well as core, high-demand platforms and services.

Wrap and retire legacy platforms with APIs ROI signals

Signals and stories you can expect to observe when applying the wrap and retire legacy platforms with APIs experiment include (but are not limited to):

- Careful and minimally risky replacement of systems that just are not able to make the jump to the benefits and options the cloud enables.
- Inertia of change can be controlled and contained as much as possible behind the anti-corruption layer APIs so that other parts of your value chains can deliver on the ROI you're looking for.

Wrap and retire legacy platforms with APIs caveats

This experiment is a compromise approach in which your existing systems are simply resisting any attempt to evolve them to gain any of the ROI from going to the cloud. This means that caveats are few and far between. If you have a legacy system that is simply never, or very unlikely ever, going to cut it in the cloud, the strangler-fig pattern is the way.[15]

Example hypothesis

Reducing a banking system to banking functionality improves speed of change and enables replacement if desired.

Over time, a core banking system had subsumed more and more crucial bank functions until any changes had unacceptably large potential blast radii. We applied the strangler-fig pattern to separate this entangled functionality at the API level and began to move those features better enabled outside of the monolith.

This move allowed us not only to improve speed of change but also to reduce our dependence on the core banking system to the point where even it could be replaced if we so desired. Though the investment was not insignificant, with this experiment we had at least enabled the possibility of replacement.

---

15 See *The Mandalorian* by Disney.

7

People, Process, and Organizational Structure

"Why are we so slow?!"

—Anonymous board member at a financial services organization

Conway's law rules,[1] period. How you organize your people will have a direct impact on how your value chains are constructed, and how they can work and be worked upon. Get it right, and your people will be the valuable differentiator you need to deliver your digitalization ROI. Get it wrong, and you could end up with less than you started with.

You could come up with the most valuable chains and supporting architecture, but if you don't organize your people in ways that help them work effectively with your architecture, then, as in a body with a strong immune system, your architectural digitalization changes will be rejected or worked around. As Ruth Malan is quoted as saying, "If the architecture of the system and the architecture of your organization are at odds, the architecture of your organization wins."[2]

The stakes could not, once again, be higher. On the one side is glorious ROI, on the other yet another painful conversation with your institution's board about "Why are we so slow NOW?!" Your hierarchical organization chart will be little help here. In fact, its archaic thinking may well be what caused the difficulties you now experience. New thinking is required to make it possible for your people to do their best work, to deliver your target digitalization ROI, supported by your architectural experiments and decisions.

---

1 Conway's law (*https://oreil.ly/_7oC5*): "Any organization that designs a system (defined broadly) will produce a design whose structure is a copy of the organization's communication structure."

2 Matthew Skelton and Manuel Pais, *Team Topologies: Organizing Business and Technology Teams for Fast Flow* (IT Revolution Press).

The Hidden Life of Teams

Working on value chains is a job for architects, software engineers, product, and oper tions. Exploring the needs of the stakeholders and turning that into the systems that cor nect to bring your value chains to life—that is the bread and butter of product-focuse software engineering. Your digitalization strategy will look primarily to improve how we your engineering teams can meet the needs of the customer. The problem is that th work is frequently undermined by three tenacious ideas: the hierarchical organizatio structure, project thinking, and a belief that the purpose of product engineering "production." This is not to be confused with the "production" environment in which th software systems that make you money operate. *Production* here refers to the challenge c making production, output, building things the purpose and focus.

PRODUCTION IS (NOT) THE PROBLEM

In *Modern Software Engineering* (Addison-Wesley Professional), Dave Farley attempted t dispel a myth that has been informing technology-enabled organizations for decade The myth that the hard part, the difficult thing to do, and so the activity that need the most attention is the production of software. More software, as much as possibl that was the answer. Write more and all will be fine. Progress is a continual march c accumulation. SLOC FTW.[3]

From the title of this section, you've probably already guessed that this is no a largely discredited view of the world. Writing code, even getting it into use, is n the hard thing, even in a highly regulated environment such as our financial service institutions. How much software you have won't define how successful you are; in fac it will quite likely hinder your success. But better *solutions* that support and unlock bette and better value chains...*that* is the job of the software engineering team.

You're not just programming, not just developing an application, but engineerin a solution. And engineering works best when it is done in a particular type of env ronment, a particular style of habitat. Great solutions come from great teams th. are aligned with clear goals and can work quickly and autonomously—teams that ar long-lived, get to know and trust each other, and are able and encouraged to combin collaborate, and learn from each other. Want to kill all this ROI? That's the job c Problem 2: hierarchical organization chart thinking.

THE PROBLEM OF HIERARCHICAL ORGANIZATION CHART THINKING

The origins of the hierarchical organization chart are occluded in the mists of histor They were possibly invented by railroad engineers, who saw an analogy in how railroad are planned from a central terminus, or born from a centurion's need to be able t visualize and order an army they couldn't see over the horizon. We're willing to bet tha the hierarchical organization chart is a mainstay, explicit or not, of almost every compan

---

3 Source lines of code for the win. The false and largely discredited idea that lines of code, specifically an increasing number of them, are the appropriate measure of productivity and progress for people building you value chains.

in the world. But when it comes to helping people do their best work on digital value chains, it is a broken view of the world. It's not just in conflict with your goals; in the hands of Conway's law, it can be downright toxic.

This is because the hierarchical organization ignores the intensity of collaboration necessary for teams to effectively work on solutions for better and better value chains. Much of your target digitalization ROI will rest on your ability to evolve your value chains quickly, and to do that, you need to create a habitat where your teams can do their jobs quickly. Hierarchy has the unfortunate effect of creating silos and divisions that directly prevent all of the qualities that your great teams need to enjoy. To have the best chance of achieving your digitalization ROI, you're going to need to bin the hierarchical, command-and-control org chart[4] and instead focus on the organizational module that enables an autonomous and highly collaborative environment for your teams.

FROM PROJECT TO PRODUCT

If everything is a project, you are focusing on the wrong thing: the work that needs to be done. Everything will be planned as tasks. Your eyes will be firmly on the ball at your feet and how well you think you're dribbling it. You'll completely lose sight of the goal, which is a delivered solution.

Worse, you will not be able to change direction, because a project often needs to be completed to manifest its value. You need to have done all the work before you get the payback. Modern Agile methods encourage a different approach, one well suited to generating innovation. Instead of focusing on how well you are progressing against a plan, Agile promotes a focus on the deliverables that help you discover the best solution.

In using an Agile approach, you are evolving a product, a node in your value chain, to better service existing needs or create new opportunities for value. Each step is a product iteration and increment that can, ideally, be verified as valuable. Each step should be as short as possible so that you can change direction when needed.[5]

The differences here are subtle but important and are best explained as a switch from *project* to *product* thinking. In project thinking, you are focusing on the work necessary to achieve a specific goal—the completion of the project. In product thinking, you are focusing on achieving small increments of value in support of a growing product.

Your teams need a long-term purpose and a sense of responsibility to work effectively and autonomously on their part of the value chain. The abstraction of project work dilutes and confuses this purpose and responsibility. On the other hand, thinking in terms of products keeps everyone's eyes on the judges' scores, not on their feet as they execute the steps of the dance.

---

4 At least in terms of how work actually gets done. These things are still useful sometimes for induction and investor audits.

5 If you can't change direction frequently based on new insights, then you're not Agile. You might be making all the right process moves, but if you can't change your mind regularly, then you might as well be working in a long-iteration plan (i.e., waterfall). That's sometimes OK if you're working on a part of a value chain that is well defined, even commoditized. But if you're looking to explore new and innovative opportunities, agility is your best bet.

WHY TEAMS?

Not sold yet? Fair enough. The main point here is that when it comes to getting the best out of your people, it is focusing on the team and how it operates that will give you the best chance of getting ROI from your digitalization strategy.

Teams are the lowest level of module for your organization. They can be constructed with just the right mix of sensitivities and skills to work autonomously across your value chains. Aligned with those chains, they can adopt product thinking, seeking the smallest product iterations and increments that achieve high-quality, secure, and reliable value as quickly as possible.

By avoiding project and hierarchical organization thinking, you can establish a collection of autonomous, responsible, and purposeful teams that can work your value chains to best effect. You will lay the foundation for Conway's law to work for you, perhaps even adopting the inverse Conway maneuver[6] to "restructur[e] your organization or team [to] prevent [your new value chains] from displaying all the same structural dysfunctions as the original." With teams as your module of choice, you can look to convert Conway's law from a source of pain to your superpower, establishing an underlying technical architecture that will enable the interactions and behaviors that will give your people the best chance to succeed.

Establishing and Evolving Your Teams

Teams are only the starting point. What teams should you have? How should they interact? How should they operate? Have we just shifted the problem from "How should your people be organized?" to "How should your teams be organized?"

There's no one-size-fits-all solution. Context is king here. However, there is lots of great guidance to help you figure out what teams you need and how you should enable and evolve their different styles of interaction over time. You can consult two resources: team topologies and Wardley Mapping.

TEAM TOPOLOGIES: TEAMS AND INTERACTION STYLES

Topologies are common in introductory IT networking courses, where they help you understand how to lay out your network and nodes to best effect. *Team topologies* work the same way; they provide a framework for how you might arrange, align, and generally lay out your teams and the networks of connection between them so they can do their work.

There is a lot to team topologies, and we give only a quick overview here.[7] At the approach's core, there are four fundamental team topologies and three foundational interaction styles to establish and evolve over time. The four fundamental team topologies are:

---

6 Not our choice of words. We blame the wonderful Jonny Leroy and Matt Simons for that one.

7 For much, much more, see *Team Topologies* by Matthew Skelton and Manuel Pais.

Stream-aligned teams
Teams aligned to the flow of work.

Enabling teams
Teams aligned to enable a capability, spread across other teams.

Complicated subsystem teams
Teams aligned to a specific, complicated, even complex, subsystem.

Platform teams
Teams aligned to provide a platform that supports the needs of other teams.

Essential team interaction modes include:

Collaboration
Two teams overlap enough in purpose for a period of time and so work very closely together.

X as a service
This is at the other end of the scale from collaboration mode. Something is consumed or shared by both teams but with minimal collaboration.

Facilitating
A team is helping or being helped by other teams.

At a given moment, a team will be moving toward a particular style and specific interaction modes with other teams, depending on what is most effective for that team's purpose. Teams in team topologies are static and long-lived, and they work with a high level of purpose and autonomy. However, their styles and interaction styles can change over time, with interaction styles being the most adaptable as new opportunities and needs to collaborate with other teams evolve.

An example might be a team responsible for creating a new payment rail, with an API frontend, that needs to interact with and depend on the core banking system. The team, or teams, responsible for the core banking system will recognize the capability being built needs to be managed and evolved as a complex subsystem, so their behaviors will align with the complex subsystem team topology. The team or teams working on the new payment rail will likely adopt behaviors characteristic of effective stream-aligned teams.

Initially, the core banking system's complex subsystem team may be encouraged to adopt a highly collaborative form of interaction mode with the new payment rail team. Then, as the needs of both parts of the value chain are understood better and mature, an X-as-a-service interaction mode may be encouraged or even emerge naturally.

Team topologies are a great taxonomy to help you establish and evolve your teams to best suit, and most effectively work on, your value chains. The four fundamental team topologies and three essential interaction modes give you a language to explore, understand, and support your teams as they seek to unlock the digitalization ROI that you seek.

WARDLEY MAPPING: EXPLORERS, VILLAGERS, AND TOWN PLANNERS

As you decide how to evolve your organization to optimally align your teams to the various parts of your value chains, exploring the right fundamental team topologies and interaction modes for your context is key. It is useful to be aware that different people, with different experience, skills, and working styles, will likely thrive, even flourish, and do their best work when focused on the elements of your chains that are aligned to their sensibilities.

Wardley Mapping[8] provides a basis for understanding these different groups of people and their sensibilities:

Explorers
> Explorers are the people most comfortable working with the unknown—with innovating quickly, turning mistakes into learnings, and moving on quickly. They'll also likely get bored working on the more stable parts of your value chains.

Villagers
> Villagers can take those novel, half-completed links in the chains and ready them for a real audience. Without the villagers, your value chains would be full of novelty and little else. The villagers take the magic and make it usable.

Town planners
> Town planners take what's usable and ready it for scale. They're the ones you want in charge of the critical, stable, and resource-intensive links in your value chains.

Crude as these characterizations may appear at first, we bet you can navigate your organization and identify different people and groups that fit these descriptions. That understanding is useful when you are looking to explore how you change up your teams.

You don't want to populate a set of teams responsible for your next novel, innovative, and differentiating AI financial trading service with people who would be best applied when that service is ready to scale. You need some teams of pioneers to forge the way, possibly organized as their own set of stream-aligned teams and working in a highly collaborative interaction mode with potentially multiple other teams.

Likewise, you don't want a team of pioneers getting bored trying to clean up a core banking account service that has become core to everything your organization does. For that, you can establish a team of settlers who will get the service ready for future town planners to move in, if or when the time comes.

Different groups of people with different sensibilities will work differently and produce different outcomes. Through understanding different types of people and their sensibilities, and considering team topologies, you will get the best out of your people, organizing them so they are aligned as effectively as possible across your current and future value chains.

---

8 Pioneers, settlers, and town planners (*https://oreil.ly/grnIt*) on Wardleypedia.

GOVERNANCE FOR TEAMS

In your newly fashioned digitalized world of ROI-delivering, autonomous, highly motivated, and value chain–aligned teams, what is the job of management and governance? Have we finally achieved a middle management–free nirvana?

No. Your role as managers and leaders of your organization is to establish and debug your teams and interaction modes as they evolve over time. As you'll see from the experiment templates in this chapter, your organization will evolve over time as you experiment with new ways to unlock your digitalization ROI at the people, process, and practice levels, as well as the architectural (see Chapter 6) and operational levels (see Chapter 8).

All of these aspects will evolve more quickly than ever before, and your job will be to ensure that your teams and their practices are set up to learn from and adapt quickly to those changing conditions to obtain, and keep obtaining, your digitalization ROI. Digitalization generates the challenge and opportunity of continuous disruption as you unlock new value chains for your business and rapidly enable it using cloud technologies, and your organization—the arrangement of your people and their topologies and interaction modes—are never "done."

People, Process, and Organizational Structure Experiment Templates

As well as looking to evolve how your people are organized toward better and better flow through team topologies, the following experiments are candidates to consider as you explore how to support your teams in unlocking digitalization ROI for your organization.

Note

Additional people, process, and organizational structure experiment templates are available for download at *https://oreil.ly/dfsac_experiments*.

EXPERIMENT TEMPLATE: OPEN COLLABORATION

As we called out at the beginning of this chapter, engineering systems is a creative endeavor that often benefits from a lot of collaboration. Nothing, absolutely no *thing*, kills collaboration faster than "find it on SharePoint." Find it. On SharePoint.

Collaboration needs tools that, as much as possible, make it *convenient* and *easy* for people to navigate, search, and collaborate inter- and intra-team. You could have the best architectural decisions, the best implementation technologies, and the people with all the best skills you need, but with one choice hinder their ability to collaborate, create, and work. And you may even lose those people, too.

This is why your choice of collaboration tools is so important, and the key characteristic is that they are *open*. Everyone in your organization can and does use them; creating is as easy as walking, and sharing information is as easy as breathing.

Often, the key is not the tool itself but the way it is set up. We picked on SharePoint earlier, and that's not really fair. SharePoint can be set up to support open, but controlled, collaboration as well as many other tools—it just frequently isn't. If the tool is heavily regimented and constrained in its usage, it will likely become a ghost town of out-of-date documents, or a trash pile that hides gems you will never, ever find. If to gain access you have to contact more than two people, and if one of them is away you cannot get that access, and when you have the access you then need to ask for a whole different set of permissions to be able to do anything, then you are *not* enabling open collaboration. If I can join your company on Day 1 and work with someone I've only just met using your tools, then you might be getting there.

Conway's law (see Chapter 6) is in effect here, too. By making it difficult for your people to engage in ad hoc collaboration, that collaboration won't happen, and this will affect the systems and value chains that you ultimately build and operate. If it's hard to work together, people frequently won't work as effectively as they could—and neither will their business units. Silos will form, and one small decision will unintentionally result in a high cost—it could even undermine your digitalization efforts completely.

This is why this next experiment is featured. In this experiment, you will look at the tools you use and, more importantly, how they are used to see how difficult they are making it for people to work together. In financial services, it's important to control access and have audit trails, but this often results in stronger, top-down restrictions than are strictly necessary from any regulatory point of view. This experiment is about doing the work to figure out just how free your organization's collaborative work can be, rather than taking the easy route of simply locking everything down.[9]

Open collaboration ROI signals

Signals and stories you can expect to observe when applying open collaboration include (but are not limited to):

- Clear inter- and intra-team collaboration
- Greater speed of change
- Faster mean time to recovery when teams collaborate on an incident
- Lower turnover of staff

Open collaboration caveats

The key caveat to this experiment is that open collaboration needs to accommodate regulatory requirements for separation of responsibilities and respect the restrictions on sharing beyond the bounds of your organization.

---

9 There are even more resources available to encourage open collaboration in the Open Practice Library (*https://openpracticelibrary.com*) and Open Organization (*https://theopenorganization.org*) initiatives.

Example hypothesis

Real-time, collaborative diagramming tools will enhance open collaboration in a hybrid work environment.

Typically during the COVID pandemic, a bank had moved its people from an office to fully remote, and as conditions eased, began looking at a hybrid approach. Several advantages and disadvantages to fully in-person and remote work settings had been uncovered, and management determined it would be beneficial for their employees to have the ability to work remotely *and* in the office.

It would be important for their engineers to be able to communicate and collaborate rapidly through diagrams, something that was done with a conference room whiteboard in the past and using various inadequate tools during the period of forced remote work.

A tool was selected that would not only allow diagrams to be created quickly and with multiple collaborators, in real time, but also to be shared, linked to, and retained in perpetuity along with a history of accountable edits.[10] Access to the tool and its results was critical and so was provided to all employees. Access could be revoked as part of the usual offboarding of personnel, but the data and history would be retained.

EXPERIMENT TEMPLATE: EXPLORE CONTINUOUS DELIVERY

Continuous delivery (CD)[11] is a staple of modern software engineering, but the term is a bit of a misnomer. The goal is not to continuously deliver *all the time* but to engineer a system such that delivery *can* happen *at any time*, thereby enabling the potential for changes to be speedily and confidently brought into production.

CD works like a forcing function, a useful constraint. By setting the goal of being able to deliver at the drop of a hat, at any point in time, many side effects are expected.

Long manual testing cycles will evolve toward faster, automated testing approaches; this is because if there is a delay of days/weeks/months to build the requisite confidence in a change, you can hardly be said to be delivering continuously. In addition, you are likely to see the advantages of automating security and reliability verifications, shifting those left (i.e., earlier in the process) so that there is minimal chance of a delivery failure and, again, ensuring that you are confident in those aspects at any time you may be asked to deliver.

Short, tightly contained deliverables may also emerge that will represent a smaller risk of change, opening the doors to greater choice and agility as to what is prioritized for delivery. DevOps practices are likely to emerge, too.

Of all the experiments you may consider, exploring continuous delivery will be one of the more impactful if you are searching for faster, more confident change and agility on a part of your value chains.

---

10 A key feature in the regulatory auditability of the system.

11 See *Continuous Delivery: Reliable Software Releases Through Build, Test, and Deployment Automation*, Jez Humble and David Farley (Addison-Wesley).

Continuous delivery ROI signals

Signals and stories you can expect to observe when applying continuous delivery include (but are not limited to):

- Impact on speed of change
- Reduction of manual work (and the associated errors) or intervention in delivery
- Greater confidence in being able to deliver
- More time spent on building business value and less on fixes

Continuous delivery caveats

Continuous delivery is a very powerful approach that will surface many difficulties you currently accept as part of the pain of delivery. Quantifying the ROI of continuous delivery is often very new in financial institutions. Your first step would be to look at how frequently you *can* deliver now, the value stream of activities that take place, and the lead time for a change to make its way into production. These are often measurements an organization has not made before, but it is important to establish their baseline so that you can then see the challenges to be overcome.

It is worth remembering that continuous delivery is often a longer-term, aspirational goal, and though just having the goal can be the driver you need for ROI to begin to emerge, those signals may not emerge at first. Like many functions of improvement, CD often surfaces pain before it surfaces benefits.

To give you even more of a taste of how such an experiment can be used in your own context, after the experiment template has been described, it will be accompanied by a collection of realistic hypotheses for financial services systems.

Example hypothesis

> Hypothesis: Applying continuous delivery to the mobile payments rail will allow us to evolve our payment rails faster.

Our digitalization target ROI includes speeding up our ability to adapt to new mobile payment rails. Mobile payment rails, particularly to frontier markets, rely on creating reliable integrations in an unreliable and rapidly changing context. By applying continuous delivery, we hope to deliver and evolve new and existing mobile payment rails quicker and with greater confidence to keep pace with these challenging contexts.

EXPERIMENT TEMPLATE: CONFIGURATION AND INFRASTRUCTURE AS CODE

It was painful enough when you had to manage configuration manually across static resources in your own data centers. Many a Friday night's plans were ruined by a subtle configuration change, made with good intent and in all innocence, that led to a catastrophic and transient problem in production. Unrepeatable and unnoticed keypresses were the cause of much chaos and stress, and now your scale, flexibility, and potential are so much higher in the cloud. Manual configuration management is no longer just a danger; at scale it becomes an impossibility.

Enter configuration and infrastructure as code. By capturing the configuration, even the infrastructural configuration, of your systems in executable code, a single source of truth on the current state of these elements in your runtime systems can be captured, understood, and carefully evolved alongside the code you already use to implement the business logic of your systems.

Configuration and infrastructure as code ROI signals

Signals and stories you can expect to observe when applying configuration and infrastructure as code include (but are not limited to):

- Greater confidence when making fundamental infrastructure and configuration changes through automation-reducing errors from manual intervention
- Ease of change audits
- Increasing the operational resilience in the cloud while keeping safe alternatives and site backup plans actionable
- Enabling platform teams to build consistent blueprints that are applied repeatably by application/product teams

Configuration and infrastructure as code caveats

While the tooling for configuration and infrastructure as code is well established in the industry, in your context, it may well require training current staff and even hiring additional staff to establish enough proficiency with the approach to see the experiment's ROI.

Example hypothesis

Treating configuration and infrastructure as code provides regulatory auditability.

An insurance company chose to adopt configuration and infrastructure as code, moving what was a collection of ad hoc and poorly documented processes and policies into the same workflow as other resources under development. In this case, all changes to configuration and infrastructure were captured in code, Ansible and Terraform in this specific case, and retained in GitHub to give a full history of review and changes.

8

Operational Models

Who's responsible for the operation of your value chain? When your value chains move from dream to critically-relied-upon, will-end-up-on-the-front-page-and-in-jail-if-wrong reality, who is accountable and responsible becomes a *very* serious question. The answer that used to be acceptable to everyone, especially financial services institutions, was to split that responsibility between those who *plan*, those who *build* or supply,[1] and those who *run*.

And that worked. When timelines for change were measured in years, and projects measured in months, handoffs between building, or engineering, and running, or operations, could be accommodated. Engineering naturally attracted developers who happily did not need to know how their stuff ran, and operations naturally attracted those who worried about little else. The world was a happy place...

...except it wasn't. This was not a friendly environment. "Can I get this past test and make it Operations' problem?" may not have been an explicit credo for software developers, but it was a tempting and evidential stance. Implicit acceptance of how the system ran as "not Development's problem" was the norm, and that understandably led to the amplification of Operations' natural tendency to be risk averse. This was especially true in financial services where regulatory, auditability, governance, and a host of other concerns sat firmly on Operations' shoulders yet could be blissfully ignored by Development.

Development was measured by change—ship it, now! Operations was measured by risk—don't ship it till you're sure! And so, with a sad inevitability, a not-so-quiet, productivity-stunting war was waged between the cubicles of every engineering department across the globe.

That was until...

---

1 In the case of third-party suppliers, such as cloud providers.

DevOps

"Fancy a coffee?" asked Bob[2] from Operations.

"Sure," said Susie from Development.

Fin

[Working title: "DevOps, an Origin Story"]

Since that heady day years ago, the DevOps movement has brought development an operations people and responsibilities together. Despite a near obsession with limitin DevOps to a vendor-led, automation toolchain and skill set, the origins of the approac were much simpler and more important. When the builders and the runners collaborate better systems arise. Breaking down the silos between development and operation enhanced the effectiveness of both groups, but why?

Focus on Flow and Feedback Loops

When Dev and Ops worked in separate silos, the two groups could build different defin tions of success. Dev would push forward, frustrated when things couldn't change fas enough, and Ops would hold back, invoking large-scale change management boards i necessary. Dev was seen as the wild west and Ops as big government. And organization wept at the ROI left on the cutting room floor by their engineering groups.

But this wasn't the only problem. There was a much more sinister issue hiding jus under the surface. Not only were the two groups most involved in delivering change an value not encouraged to work together, but they also couldn't *learn* together. Lesson learned in Operations stayed in Operations, even through the people who could learn th most from those lessons were the developers.

To overcome dysfunction, many Jira boards were created, and largely ignored. Con tinuous improvement committees were formed to shuffle tickets from one backlog t another, cleverly assuring everyone that lessons were being learned and follow-up action to solve problems were being tracked. Special categories were created to explain wha these issues were, such as technical debt, reliability, versioning, or security vulnerabil ties. The air gap between Dev and Ops was where those backlogs went to die.

Bringing Dev and Ops together changed that, too. Now both groups could be hel to the same powerful metrics of what good, even great, should look like. Metrics such a those captured by the DevOps Research and Assessment team (DORA)[3] could align th need for speed with the need for reliability, including the four core metrics of:

---

2 The names have been changed to protect the wonderful.

3 Not to be confused with the Digital Operational Resiliency Act; see *The 2019 Accelerate State of DevOps* (*https://oreil.ly/huQwT*) and *Accelerate: Building and Scaling High Performing Technology Organizations* by Nicole Forsgren, Jez Humble, and Gene Kim.

Deployment frequency
How often you can successfully perform a release to production.

Lead time for changes
The amount of time it takes a change to get into production.

Change failure rate
The percentage of deployments causing a failure in production.

Time to restore service
How long it takes you to recover from a failure in production.

With joint metrics, a balance could be found among these metrics to determine what good should look like, entirely avoiding the cold war of conflicting Dev and Ops goals. And then the magic happened. With the disappearance of the wall between Dev and Ops, the feedback loops of learning became free to reach the people who could really do something about those lessons. No more were important actions from incidents able to hide in perpetuity in never-read incident reports or dusty Jira backlogs. Working together, Dev and Ops could understand and do something about those issues. They could share the learning. They could.

But then there is financial services and *segregation of duties*.

YOU BUILD IT, YOU RUN IT...YOU GO TO JAIL?!

When computer scientist Werner Vogels coined the phrase "You build it, you run it" in 2016 (*https://oreil.ly/R-6Fx*), he was likely thinking of the agency that cloud resources give you. Through the power of utility and hyperscale commodity cloud providers, you really could build and run your own systems, and given the advantages mentioned above, that would enhance the quality of the services you supply.

But in financial services, as well as other regulated domains, there is a contrary rule of segregation of duties (*https://oreil.ly/yIw2u*). The idea is that by keeping walls between the person responsible for one activity and someone who does another activity, no one can seize and maliciously manipulate the whole activity end to end. In financial services, this results in the creation of *deliberate* silos to ensure that activities such as money laundering and other fraudulent behavior are difficult, if not impossible.

SEGREGATION DOESN'T MEAN ZERO COLLABORATION

On the face of it, Werner and the rule of segregation of duties seem fundamentally in conflict. If DevOps encourages, and cloud services enable, the ability for one team to build and run their own systems, but good regulatory governance says you can't, regulatory is likely to win. When faced with penalties, jail, or even being shut down,[4] DevOps be damned.

---

4 The main fear of shareholders, after all.

But not so fast. If we go back to the original point of DevOps, which was to encourage collaboration and important feedback loops, we can achieve those things while also restricting who can actually *do* what. Dev and Ops can build a working relationship in a financial services institution, but, depending on the value chain and its regulatory implications, the two may not be able to collaborate *within* a team. Rather they need to collaborate *between* teams. The team topologies and interaction styles from Chapter 7 entirely support this. Financial services institutions can get the benefits of DevOps and stay comfortably within the rules of the regulator.

The realization that DevOps and segregation of duties, along with other regulatory control strategies, can coexist is a game changer. Without DevOps, it would be difficult, even impossible, to unlock the ROI of many of the advantages of modern software and systems engineering. DevOps, along with the focus on continuous, reliable delivery that is encouraged through the DORA metrics, is the foundation for unlocking your digitalization ROI.

Operational Models Experiment Templates

Navigating possible experiments with operational models can pay quick dividends, or hide latent problems. Choosing wisely and staying close to any experiment that directly affects how your systems operate is the best way to mitigate the risk of change, and, as always, it's important to keep in mind that any experiment is a step into the unknown and so needs to be carefully assessed for impact in your unique context.

Note

An additional operational models experiment template is available for download at *https://oreil.ly/dfsac_experiments*.

EXPERIMENT TEMPLATE: SURFACE EVERYTHING WITH OBSERVABILITY

"You see, but you do not observe."

—Sherlock Holmes, in "A Scandal in Bohemia" by Sir Arthur Conan Doyle

In the cloud, everything is changing, all the time. Even if your systems are not evolving, the conditions in which they operate likely are. Traditional dashboards, metrics, and monitoring still work, but they won't give you the pre-canned answers you need to make the best decisions to take advantage of this dynamic environment.

This is where observability comes in. *Observability* encourages you to surface as many signals as possible from your value chains to help you understand emergent system behavior. Observability encourages you to enable and enrich this signal feed to the point where you can detect knowns, even known unknowns, and you're able to ask entirely unanticipated questions knowing you have the raw data to get the answers. You're not limited to close-ended questions anticipated in advance; with observability you can ask new, open-ended questions that provide all the information you need to comprehend, even debug, your systems in production.

Observability ROI signals

Signals and stories you can expect to see when applying observability include (but are not limited to):

- Speedily and collaboratively debugging systems across value chains, teams, and systems
- A foundation for system verification, testing conditions in production
- Fundamentally changing the team's mindset toward a data-driven culture

Observability caveats

Observability requires a new approach, set of tools, and even mindset from that of traditional management and monitoring. While it's quite an investment, it is also a key foundational source of intelligence on your runtime system performance, useful for optimization efforts as well as forecasting needs, and it underpins many of the other possible experiments in this category.

Example hypothesis

Observability promotes confident and speedy debugging across value chains.

In the past, debugging across payment systems, through core banking systems, and back again was a challenge of Tolkienian proportions. Requiring a small army of people, tracing what happened just now, let alone yesterday or last week, was difficult in the extreme. Implementing observability by applying open telemetry was explored to improve the mean time to recovery of systems during planned and unplanned incidents.

EXPERIMENT TEMPLATE: SITE RELIABILITY ENGINEERING

In financial services, trust is everything and reliability builds trust. Reliability here is measured ultimately by whether your customers and other stakeholders can *rely* on your value chains to deliver according to their expectations. For this reason, reliability is essentially a question of ROI: What investment must be made to meet those expectations?

Site reliability engineering (SRE) is an approach to answering that question. The answer will help to prioritize work based on balancing reliability improvements against product feature development. SRE, originally coined by Google Engineering's Ben Treynor Sloss, takes reliability from an aspiration to an engineering problem with a clear framework as to how to decide when, and how much, to invest in reliability.

Site or Service?

SRE came from Google, where Google's reliability was captured and measured based on the reliability of the Google site. As SRE has developed, its meaning has broadened to include any service that is provided to users. This could be an internal service within a value chain or an externally facing API or website.

The first word of the three-letter acronym is not the most important one. SRE helps you prioritize and deliberately engineer for an appropriate level of reliability, so the second and third letters are the emphasis.

At the heart of SRE are two concepts:

Service level objectives (SLOs)
Your SLOs are the target levels of measurable performance for a service to be declared reliable (i.e., to meet the expectations of the users of that service). A typical example would be for a service to be 99.9% available (i.e., producing an expected response in a timely manner).

Error budgets
If an SLO defines the acceptable level of performance, error budgets declare what disruption or deviation is acceptable to the service's users. Referring to the example above, 99.9% uptime as an SLO would indicate that you can have an error budget of 0.1%.

SLOs should be measurable, ideally automatically, through service level indicators (SLIs). SLIs are empirical measurements of the behavior of the service that underpin an SLO and provide tracking and trends for your SLOs over time. SLIs are sometimes said to *cover* an SLO, as in "A set of SLIs provides measurable *coverage* of an SLO."

Error budgets highlight that there is an *acceptable* amount of deviation in any system such that the user is still happy. This is important as it sets the risk level for the service. Without an error budget, it is implied that a service should always be available and, given that the service may be evolving and other transient, turbulent conditions[5] out of your control will and do occur, this standard is at best naive and at worst just plain impossible.

The combination of SLOs and error budgets provides reliability signals that can help you decide when to invest in improving reliability (i.e., when error budgets are consistently blown). Options are to invest in reducing manual, repeatable work—referred to

---

5 A long-winded way of saying "reality."

as *toil*[6] in SRE—through automation, paying back some technical debt,[7] and essentially prioritizing work that brings your error budget back under control.

What About Service Level Agreements?

SLAs predate SRE and are contractually agreed obligations, promises, as to the service level a user can expect of the service they consume and you provide. When an SLA is not met, you have an unhappy user and possibly a compensation conversation on your hands.

SLOs are objectives you, as the provider of the service, set. They are usually higher bars than your SLAs as your user should not be on the telephone threatening legal action for a blown error budget. You can think of your SLOs and Error Budgets being what you have to play with while still having happy users. SLAs are the measure of when your user becomes unhappy enough that they will start to look at what you contractually agreed to provide.

SRE ROI signals

SRE is *all about* ROI, provides a decision-making framework for deciding when to invest in reliability. The signals you can look for are the same as the results of practicing SRE, better reliability across your value chains and happier users of those chains.

SRE caveats

SRE requires a commitment to and discipline in application of empirical measurement, especially when it comes to creating and measuring your SLOs, setting your Error Budgets, and following through on the signals that those concepts give you. SRE on its own won't make your value chains more reliable; the decisions you make on the back of its signals will do that. For that reason it is useful to create a clear error budget policy that declares what needs to happen when your error budgets are acutely or chronically blown.

---

6 Not to be confused with *time off in lieu*. Toil here denotes work that is manual, repeatable, and probably error prone and painful. Time off in lieu is a welcome recovery period after you've had to go above and beyond on some activity.

7 See the excellent book *Your Code as a Crime Scene: Use Forensic Techniques to Arrest Defects, Bottlenecks, and Bad Design in Your Programs* by Adam Tornhill (Pragmatic Bookshelf) for more on capturing and working on technical debt in your systems.

Example hypothesis

Introducing SLOs and error budgets will reduce manual on-call work.

On-call work is killing the productivity of the teams responsible for evolving a critica banking service or value chain. Fires are being fought instead of features being deve oped, and the users are noticing. Adopting SRE surfaces the right signals to prom addressing all this TOIL as part of the work prioritization negotiations, i.e. backlo refinement, for those teams.

EXPERIMENT TEMPLATE: FINOPS

If DevOps invited operations to the table, and DevSecOps (see Chapter 7) did the sam to encourage close collaboration and fast feedback loops with the security folks as wel FinOps is not surprisingly going to bring another group to the same table: financ Specifically, you gain financial awareness of the cost of running the services, softwar and systems that form your value chains.

FinOps surfaces, distributes, and ultimately shares the cost of running your system across everyone involved in working on and providing those systems. If you write it an run it, you're now also financially accountable for its ROI.

Similar to SRE, FinOps provides a set of tools and a decision-making framework t help everyone pay attention to how money is being spent to provide your value chain This is especially important when those value chains are moving toward public clou services where there is the potential for careful cost reductions, and enormous co overruns, at the flip of a virtual switch. In the cloud, your static, fixed expenditures ca be largely removed in favor of flexible operational expenditures. When resources ca be obtained and discarded in minutes, even seconds,[8] and as many of the decision need to be made as close to the value chains as possible, annual budgetary controls wi creak. Instead, adopting a FinOps approach will give you the power to make these new dynamic financial characteristics of your value chains visible.

Bringing financial awareness to your teams using FinOps turns the cost of runnin your value chains from something largely secret—with teams being blissfully unaware the cost of what they produce—but safe. Costs are now visible to everyone, so they ca factor cost into their solutions and priorities.

The Power and (Financial) Pain of Freedom of Scale in the Cloud

We'd decided to spin up a demo for a board at a large financial institution, to be run for only a few hours, during a talk followed by a discussion. We used the power of a public cloud to show not only how we could quickly and easily provision the resources we needed but also how we could scale

---

8 For example, function as a service (FaaS) styles of implementation are often measured in numbers of requests, or function invocations, and compute seconds.

to extremely large capacity almost as quickly, with only our finances holding us back.

The discussion was great, and the evening was judged a success. Until three weeks later when the cloud bill arrived. In all the excitement of the discussion and the possibilities for the value chains in the financial institution, we'd forgotten one important task: to switch off the high-scale demo. We had no FinOps signals or controls to warn us and no auto-scaling to do the work on our behalf. This was a hard lesson in the power and potential for the cloud to provide everything, but at a cost, and we became proponents of FinOps from then on.

FinOps ROI signals

Just like SRE, FinOps is *all about* enabling ROI decisions from the cost point of view. If controlling and optimizing cost, thereby improving profitability, is what you seek, FinOps is the way to do it in a highly collaborative way that embraces the dynamic nature of the cloud.

FinOps caveats

Calculating costs is hard, and calculating costs on public, hyperscale clouds is *very* hard. Complicated pricing structures and fluid potential for facilities such as spot pricing can make just obtaining the right accountable signals a lot of work in its own right. Tooling is improving rapidly here but, at the moment, that tooling tends to focus on cloud infrastructure costs alone.

Things become even more complicated when you have shared cloud resources across value chains. How do you intend to distribute this cost? In a multi or hybrid cloud environment, how do you come up with the figures necessary to underpin your FinOps decision making? These are all significant challenges to adopting FinOps, but the ROI is often large enough to warrant the investment. It's good for accurate accounting anyway, even if you are not going the full route towards shared responsibility that FinOps advocates.

Example hypothesis

Using FinOps and SRE together will help evaluate different solutions for both reliability and cost.

When two or more solutions are on the table, applying FinOps and SRE together provides the dynamic signals necessary to quickly verify, and even suggest alternative, solutions to generate a value chain.

9

Exploring Paths, Destination Unknown

"To improve is to change; to be perfect is to change often."

—*Prime Minister Winston Churchill, when asked why he'd changed his mind*

Risk. All change comes with risk, and as people involved in providing financial services, no one is more aware of the burden of trust that falls on our shoulders than we are. Risk is our bread and butter, and with no risk, there is no return. No risk of pain, no opportunity for gain, and if you're going to harness the benefits of transforming your value chains to take advantage of the age of cloud, change is potentially massive—as is the potential for pain.

Baby steps are the key to building and executing a successful cloud digitalization strategy. You want to take small, experimental, highly reflective steps toward the signals of ROI that everyone knows are being sought. If a step is big, question and analyze it until you can make it small. If it looks impossible to do without everything, everywhere, all at once, you've not explored it enough.

Can You Stop (and Still Have Gained Value)?

Each step on your digitalization journey, while being experimental, should deliver valuable increments. Even if the only value you get is the insight that a particular step did *not* deliver any signals of the ROI you're hoping to move toward, that's an ROI in itself. You've surfaced new information to feed back through your Observe, Orient, Decide, and Act (OODA) loop to redirect your efforts elsewhere, and that's a win. Your steps might be tiny, but each one carries the weight of value in what it *tells* you, as much as what change it *delivers*.

Crafting your digitalization journey in small, iterative, and incremental ROI signal–seeking steps has an added benefit that isn't obvious at first glance. Not only can you keep going on that journey for as long as you are seeking your ROI, but you can also *choose to stop* at any time and you will have made gains. Every step can be a call to carry on, or it can be a moment to reflect and stop, knowing you have achieved something whenever that decision is made.

There's a simple acid test for whether you have the capacity to make the important decision to stop your digitalization. If you find yourself reviewing your planned steps or experiments and changes and you don't see anything of value, anything that empowers you to stop, for months, then work needs to be done. Executing and steering a digitalization program should be something that is easy to get started, as only the first few steps need to be agreed upon and approved, and simple to stop, as value *will* have been achieved at any moment in time.

Continuous Delivery and the Ability to Stop

Using the question "Can you stop (and still have gained value)?" to challenge the granularity of your work in executing your digitalization strategy is closely related to, and inspired by, the practice of continuous delivery (CD). CD has a similar question that you can use as a forcing factor to judge how well you are practicing continuous delivery: "Can you deliver, right now?"

When asked "Can you deliver, now?" if at any time the answer is, more often than not, a nervous "No!" then this is a reminder that your processes and gates are maybe not as lean and trusted as they need to be really continuously delivering. Continuous delivery means you can deliver at any moment in time, at the drop of a hat. Your tightly value-centric digitalization plan offers the same freedom by being able to stop at the drop of an entirely different hat.

Stop When Done, for Risk, or for Change

If a well-constructed digitalization journey is broken into small baby steps of valuable insight or change, then you can stop at any time. But why would you stop?

You might stop, slow down, or even backtrack for the same reasons that a product stops being evolved. You may achieve the value you were looking for, so one strand of your digitalization push can be ticked off. Conversely, you might encounter an experimental insight that identifies a risk that is such a blocker to a needed ROI that you decide the mountain ahead is too high. So you can stop then too, before you expend a lot of resources on trying to achieve base camp.

Finally, you can revisit and abandon planned steps quickly and easily if you can achieve a high degree of isolation between each of your journey's steps. There is still value in deciding that what you were planning to explore, experiment with, and change is highly unlikely to deliver any of the evolving ROI signals you are looking for. Even your ROI can change, and the cheapest option is always to abandon the plan rather than carry on regardless because you think you have to, because of perceived sunk cost[1] and the failure so far to realize any ROI.

Optimize for (Frequent) Learning

A good digitalization roadmap is resilient, which means it is constantly evolving as new information comes to light (see "Experiment Template: Engineer Resilience" on *https://oreil.ly/dfsac_experiments*). Your digitalization roadmap plots careful, small steps to seek a black cat in a dark room; that is, your ROI is obscured by the complexity of your organization's sociotechnical habitat of value chains. Gradually, a consistent platform infrastructure can emerge that supports foundations already established through experimentation, opening the landscape to further ROI-seeking experimentation.

Meeting with stakeholders frequently to adjust, steer, and otherwise compare your plans with reality is the main governance activity of your digitalization. You're not there just to project manage a delivery; you're there to steer a research and development program.

Tying the Room Together

Navigating all the potential experiments and ROI, harnessing all the potential of cloud technologies, and enabling all the potential of your people is the name of your digitalization game. You'll be enabling and amplifying the potential your organization already has.

As shown in Figure 9-1, it is through tight OODA loops, clear and challenged value chains, a broad range of experiments, and changes made tentatively because you understand the natural complexity in your habitat, you will construct and navigate toward the ROI delivered by the cloud that your financial services organization deserves.

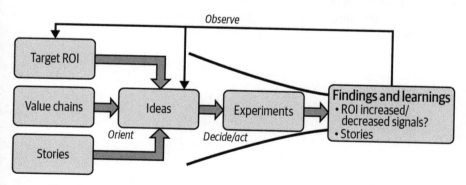

Figure 9-1. Your digitalization roadmap is a sequence of experiments, ideally decoupled, that help you steer transformation by seeking ROI signals and stories.

---

1 "One of the most commonly cited human irrationalities is the sunk-cost fallacy, in which people continue to invest in a losing venture because of what they have invested so far rather than in anticipation of what they will gain going forward," Steven Pinker, *Rationality: What It Is, Why It Seems Scarce, Why It Matters* (Penguin Books).

Continuous Digitalization

We've talked a lot in this chapter about the power to stop, but that doesn't mean yo
have to, or that many organizations do. When you establish a digitalization culture c
carefully seeking ROI using experiments to guide how to transform your value chain
and business processes, then it's common to lose sight of a discrete, clean endpoint t
your efforts.

But why do you need an endpoint? If you're gaining ROI and there's no end i
sight, why stop? This is why we think of digitalization, especially digitalization in th
age of cloud where there is such a profusion of possibilities to explore, as a produc
and not a project. Digitalization is not time bound—it is not a transient exercise. Yo
are not seeking ROI through transformation today and not tomorrow. There may be
beginning, but there doesn't have to be an end. "No more ROI please" is a rare busines
decision.

Given the disruption manifesting in the climatic conditions covered in Chapter 4
and as new climatic forces surface, digitalization can end up being a program of continu
ous improvement and ROI seeking, and that's OK! Digitalization is transforming you
business and systems to take full advantage of technologies such as those in the cloud
and we are just at the beginning of realizing how much potential there is in thes
technologies. The road ahead is full of peril and opportunity in at least equal measure
and your digitalization strategy will be a key, ongoing part of your organization's journe
into the future.

The opportunities for scale, new and better value chains, increased agility, carefu
data governance and durability, gains in operational excellence and efficiency, security
reliability, and availability are only increasing. Those who explore and learn fastest wi
win. Through your digitalization, you place yourself squarely on the right side of tha
challenge and opportunity. With your digitalization strategy, we don't think you'll need it
Good luck!

Index

About the Authors

Jamil Mina is the Head of the Regional Office of Technology, Financial Services, at Red Hat. A 25+ year technology veteran in the financial services industry, Jamil is passionate about the value of open source and how it can help financial institutions be successful in achieving their digital transformation objectives. His areas of expertise include security, risk, and compliance; DevOps practices; open hybrid cloud; and banking and financial systems architecture.

Previously, Jamil was a leader at BMO Financial Group, a large financial institution in Canada and in the top 50 worldwide. During his tenure, he enabled continuous deployment, data center automation, and container orchestration. Driving such complex transformational capabilities required a strong collaboration with the business and application development teams.

Armin Warda is the FSI EMEA Chief Technologist at Red Hat. He supports Red Hat's financial services customers and partners in the adoption of Red Hat technology, particularly in regard to operational efficiency, security, and compliance as well as on their journey to hybrid cloud. He is currently exploring the impact of proposed European regulations and initiatives on the financial services industry and their IT providers, such as the Digital Operational Resiliency Act (EU-DORA) and the Artificial Intelligence Act (EU-AIA). Among his areas of interest are also environment, social and governance (ESG) aspects of IT, trustworthy AI, and the potential transformation of the payment industry through the introduction of StableCoins by big tech companies and central bank digital currencies (CBDCs) as currently being discussed by central banks around the world, the EU, and G7.

Armin has recently joined Red Hat. Prior to his current role, he worked for 22 years at Postbank Systems as a Senior IT Architect for Postbank and Deutsche Bank. Armin holds a master's degree in computer science from the Technical University of Dortmund.

Rafael Marins is a tech executive passionate about open source innovation, drawing from his extensive software development, entrepreneurship, and management background. His expertise has significantly influenced the strategic tech choices of large enterprises, including those in the financial sector. Rafael offers valuable guidance on technology roadmaps, architecture, governance, enterprise integration, business model design, digitalization, and cloud strategies. With over 25 years of experience across multiple industries, he currently works globally as a Portfolio Product Marketing Manager at Red Hat.

Rafael has earned a master's in business administration from the Pontifical Catholic University of Rio Grande do Sul and a bachelor's in business administration from the Universidade Veiga de Almeida. As a founding member of the OW2 Consortium, he has also launched various open source projects and presented at international tech conferences. Most recently, he has made notable contributions to the Banking Industry Architecture Network (BIAN) association, including the Coreless Banking initiative and chairing the Event-Driven Architecture working group.

Russ Miles is on a mission, as an author, speaker, and engineering manager, to help people thrive in one of the harshest, and potentially impactful, working environments: software system engineering.

Through his books, mentorship, open source contributions, talks, courses, and daily work, Russ tries to help people who are responsible for building and running some of today's most critical software-based systems to develop their own and their team's grit, resilience, antifragility, psychological safety, EQ, and empathy to flourish at work and in their lives.

Russ can be reached by email at *russ@russmiles.com*, on LinkedIn, and on Twitter.

Colophon

The cover image is by Susan Thompson. The cover fonts are Guardian Sans and Gilroy. The text font is Scala Pro and the heading font is Benton Sans.

Ingram Content Group UK Ltd.
Milton Keynes UK
UKHW022353100523
421542UK00006B/12